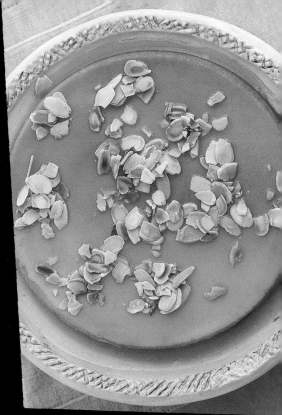

CLOCKWISE FROM
TOP LEFT:

SKEWERED LAMB
WITH RIOJA RED
WINE VINAIGRETTE

POMEGRANATE
GRANITA AND FRESH
PINEAPPLE ICES

POTATO AND
CASCABEL—CRUSTED
HALIBUT WITH
MANGO-CARROT
BROTH AND MANGO—
GREEN ONION SALSA

TOASTED
ALMOND FLAN

CARAMELIZED
FIG TART

CURRIED SHELLFISH
AND CHICKEN PAELLA

GRILLED TUNA
MARINATED IN
ROMESCO FLAVORS
WITH MELTED
LEEKS AND ONIONS
AND OVEN-DRIED
TOMATO OIL

Bobby Flay's

From My Kitchen To Your Table

BY **BOBBY FLAY** AND **JOAN SCHWARTZ**

PHOTOGRAPHS BY **TOM ECKERLE**

DESIGN BY **ALEXANDER ISLEY INC.**

 CLARKSON POTTER/PUBLISHERS
NEW YORK

BABY CLAMS STEAMED
IN GREEN ONION BROTH

COOL PLATTERS TABLE

"M

1

MENU

SAFFRON RICE SALAD
WITH SWEET AND
FIERY DRESSING

y table is

CARPACCIO
OF BEEF WITH
OREGANO
VINAIGRETTE,
ARUGULA, AND
MANCHEGO
CHEESE

SPICY JUMBO LUMP
CRABMEAT AND
BLACK BEAN SALAD
WITH ROASTED
RED PEPPER SAUCE
AND CILANTRO OIL

RED AND YELLOW
GAZPACHO WITH
GRILLED SEA SCALLOPS

like

W

ith the

HONEY-RUM BAKED
BLACK BEANS

YELLOW CORN-COATED
SOFTSHELL CRABS WITH RED
CHILE-MUSTARD SAUCE

CABBAGE AND GREEN BEAN SALAD

**FRESH GREEN PEA AND TOASTED
CORIANDER RISOTTO**

10

SEA SCALLOP CEVICHE WITH
GRILLED RED ONION AND
MANGO-TORTILLA SALAD

GRILLED STEAK
WITH GARLIC
AND HOT PEPPER
MARINADE

GRILLED PLANTAINS
WITH SPICY BROWN
SUGAR GLAZE

ar

LEMON-THYME RICE

omas.

GARLIC AND OREGANO-MARINATED GRILLED CHICKEN WITH GRILLED PEPPER AND BLACK OLIVE RELISH

FOLLOWING PAGES:

SQUID, FRIED PLANTAIN, AND MANGO SALAD WITH FRESH MINT

GRILLED ZUCCHINI WITH ROMESCO SAUCE

CILANTRO RICE

and flavors of

MENU

OVEN-ROASTED PORK TENDERLOIN
WITH BLACK OLIVE TAPINADE AND
CHARRED YELLOW PEPPER SAUCE

kinds of

GROUPER ROASTED IN BANANA LEAVES
WITH ORANGE-PINEAPPLE RELISH

dishes.

OVEN-ROASTED
WILD MUSHROOMS
WITH GOAT CHEESE
AND CHILE OIL

SAFFRON-TOMATO RICE

all together

melding

her."

Why make
a meal that
you can't enjoy
along with
everyone else?

Let me introduce you to food that is fun.

Dedication

IN MEMORY OF MY GRANDMOTHER, MARY FLAY, WHOSE HOLIDAY TABLES WERE FILLED WITH UNDENIABLE LOVE AND THE BEST FOOD ON EARTH, AND TO THE ARRIVAL OF MY DAUGHTER, SOPHIE FLAY. WHAT COULD BE BETTER? B.F.

TO ALLEN, DAVID, RACHEL, AND DEBORAH, WHO PROVIDE THE ESSENTIAL INGREDIENTS: LOVE AND LAUGHTER. J.S.

Acknowledgments

I'm grateful to everyone who contributed to the success of this book, directly and indirectly. My deep and special thanks to:

DOROTHY FLAY and **BILL FLAY,** my parents. How did you guys survive it?

LAURENCE KRETCHMER, business partner and great friend, who's always there for me.

JERRY KRETCHMER and **JEFF BLISS,** for their enthusiasm and constant encouragement.

WAYNE BRACHMAN, executive pastry chef of my restaurants and catering company, who helps in the development of every dessert, cookie, ice cream, pie crust, bread, and roll. Basically, Wayne's the best!

STEPHANIE BANYAS, my personal and business assistant, who finds all my mistakes and fixes them.

JOAN SCHWARTZ, my co-author, who always understands. Without her magic pencil, this book would only be a dream.

JANE DYSTEL, literary agent extraordinaire. Thanks for being on the front line.

ALEX ISLEY, the most incredible graphic artist in the world.

TOM ECKERLE, whose food photography is second to none.

CECI GALLINI, whose prop styling could make anyone's risotto look great.

ROY FINAMORE, editor. He does it his way. Thanks for a great book.

FRAN BERNFELD, who always has the right thing to say.

CRAIG PETROFF, who keeps the dining room at Mesa Grill humming.

CHRIS HEWITT, chef de cuisine at Mesa Grill, for being able to absorb the immense pressures of his position and creating a wonderful working atmosphere.

NEIL MANACLE, the talented former chef at Bolo, who executed and responded to my every whim— well, almost every whim.

SCOTT HENCKLE, who keeps Bolo's Spanish beat at fever pitch.

LARRY MANHEIM, who has gone from spoonbread to chef/partner of BF Catering. It's great to have you in my corner.

LISA DEAN, my catering director, a person who will achieve anything she wants to achieve.

JAMES BREULER, chef at Mesa City, who keeps it all together and always knows what "time" it is.

PETER MENDELSOHN, for his commitment and dedication to Mesa City.

MANNY GATDULA, controller, who makes sure all the bills get paid.

STACY DEMPSEY, for keeping our costs in line.

BARBARA BOGART, for her professionalism, food sense, and upbeat personality.

ANDREW BARDES, for his "want-it-all" attitude and bad stock picks.

RICK PITCHER, for his willingness to adapt.

NICOLE REISMAN, my former assistant who helped get this book off the ground and whose enthusiasm kept me striving for more.

STEVEN KALT, not just a great chef—a great cook.

JERRY AND JANET SILVERSTEIN, my greatest customers.

JACK MCDAVID, longtime friend. Keep on chillin'.

PATRICK O'BRIEN—Spielberg, beware!

New Yo

New York is an exciting food city, where nearly every ethnic culture is represented on every level. It's hometown, and it's been the major influence in my career because of the great chefs I've been able to work with and learn from and, just as important, because of the accessibility of really fine restaurants.

I remember, back in 1987, eating at a place on the Upper East Side called Mezzaluna, where I found exciting ingredients like arugula, radicchio, fresh herbs, and white truffle oil. One evening, I was enjoying a carpaccio of beef with arugula and Parmesan cheese, and the waiter came over to drizzle some extra-virgin olive oil over it. At the same time, I was buttering a piece of bread. Suddenly, a hand reached over my shoulder and grabbed my wrist. It was Francesca Cianchi, the restaurant manager, a formidable and passionate advocate of perfection in food. "Bobby," she said, "why would you eat extra-virgin olive oil from Italy and combine it with butter from Wisconsin?" I learned an important lesson at that dinner: Every food has its own time and place. There's nothing wrong with rich Wisconsin butter, but it should never compete with light, fruity Italian olive oil. I also learned that the fresh, healthy fare of the Mediterranean was here to stay—but it would be a while before I was ready to make that food my own.

I moved up through the culinary ranks, learning and working in trend-setting restaurants like Bud's, Hulot's, and Miracle Grill. In January 1991, Mesa Grill opened its doors with me as chef and partner. That restaurant offered New Yorkers the food of the American Southwest—bold, full-flavored dishes—in a lively, contemporary, high-energy atmosphere. By November 1993, it was clear we had a successful restaurant that was getting better and better. It was time to explore something new.

After a lot of thought and research, I realized that Spain was the forgotten country as far as New York food was concerned. Of course, there were Spanish restaurants in Manhattan, but they seemed to be either the red-and-white-checked tablecloth variety or the high-end "French-service" type. Spain meant something entirely different to me: it meant Barcelona, where there was always a buzz of excitement as people gathered to enjoy great Latin food and Spanish sherries and sangrias. Barcelona and New York seemed to me a perfect fit, and that was it—Bolo was born!

At Bolo, I have been able to reinterpret the Mediterranean foods that inspired me earlier in my career, to emphasize their Latin accents (which include Cuban and Mexican as well as Spanish), and to highlight their bold flavors. These are the very same foods you will find in this book: tender codfish in a crisp almond crust, served with preserved oranges and spicy orange vinaigrette; sweet baby clams steamed in herbal, garlicky green onion broth; flavorful pan-roasted rabbit accented with a sweet and spicy sauce of crushed blackberries and ancho chiles; steaming risotto perfumed with saffron and topped with juicy grilled shrimp; grilled tuna infused with the flavors of a romesco sauce—fresh tomatoes, chile peppers, garlic, olive oil, vinegar, and nuts—served over a melting sauté of leeks and onions; creamy rich flans, puddings, and ice creams; and refreshing sangrias based on peaches and pomegranates.

In your home, exciting dishes like these will bring people together and set the stage for informal good times. I will tell you how to prepare them so that you, your family, and your friends all can share them around your own table. This book is about enjoying good company and wonderful food, and, perhaps most important, it's all about flavor!

Bobby Flay
New York City

Introd

Whenever you prepare a special meal for friends or family, two important factors guide each choice you make: flavor and attitude. Your party will be defined by the food you cook and by the spirit you create. And if you follow my suggestions, both will be marked by exuberance, boldness, and fun.

Latin flavors make my dishes exciting, but this book won't limit you to any single Latin country or tradition. Cilantro, capers, and codfish are equally at home in Spain, Mexico, or Cuba, so it's easy to take an ingredient from one classic national dish and match it with something from another place. That's why I give Mexican tamales a sweet stuffing of Cuban plantains; I bathe grilled tuna in Mexican mole sauce, traditionally served with chicken; I serve squid, popular in Spain, in a salad with Cuban plantain chips and mangoes, and Mexican chipotles and cilantro; and I marinate zucchini in a Spanish romesco sauce enlivened with Mexican chiles.

As for attitude, the next time you entertain, take a big, bold step and forget about serving separate courses. Instead, set out an array of lively, colorful dishes all at the same time and tell your guests to try them in any order they choose. (There's more about this in the next chapter, "Getting It All Together.")

The chapters that follow, like the recipes themselves, discard the old idea of dividing meals into courses. Nothing is clearly an accompaniment, an appetizer, or a main course: it's all just food. Since everything is served at the same time, the chapters indicate where the dishes have been cooked—"From the Oven," "From the Grill," "From the Stovetop"—or how they are served—"Cool Platters." Rice dishes; vinaigrettes, oils, sauces, and relishes; and desserts rate their own chapters. All the recipes are planned for casual, family-style meals that will serve eight very generously—and probably give you some ● leftovers for tomorrow.

uction

Tips from Bobby's Kitchen

1 When you use an ingredient, you want to taste it, so don't sprinkle on a bit of oregano, or cilantro, or ancho chile powder—throw in a lot! Let spicy, salty, sweet, and sour flavors jump out at you from dishes accented with chile peppers, capers, fruits, herbs, and vinegars.

2 More often than not, you can turn the heat up high, whatever cooking method you are using. Let the grill, the oven, the stovetop get very hot. When you sauté foods, wait until the oil in the pan starts smoking—or until the ceiling begins to turn gray. Searing over high heat seals in flavors and juices and so gives food contrasting textures: crisp outside, tender and moist inside.

3 Use a little salt and pepper with everything—salads, meat, fish, vegetables—to draw out the natural flavors and bring them together. If you sauté a great fillet of snapper with no seasonings, it will taste like nothing much. When you season just a bit, all of a sudden you start tasting the sweetness of the fish.

4 Water is an important ingredient because it is neutral, adding no flavor. It also evens out the consistency of a dish. Use it to thin sauces, steam foods, and cook risotto. (If you keep adding stock to risotto as it cooks, the flavor concentrates and you may get more than you want. Add a little water instead.)

5 Keep tasting food as you prepare it and taste the finished dish one last time before you put it on the plate. If you're not chewing, you're not cooking.

6 Use cast-iron pans—my favorite kind—especially when you want to get a beautiful sear on a steak or a piece of fish. They last forever and are very affordable.

7 The secret to getting everything on the table at the same time is to prioritize. When you cook, start with those elements that take the longest and do them the night before or early in the morning of your dinner. Do as many things ahead as you can: a vinaigrette or sauce can easily wait in the refrigerator, as can cleaned and cooked squid, washed greens, or fried plantains. Even a risotto can be started early and finished at the last minute.

Ingredients

BANANA LEAVES, DRIED	Use to wrap fish for roasting. They give a subtle flavor to the foods they wrap. The leaves are large, so cut them into usable pieces and store in the freezer. You can buy them at Hispanic markets. Dried cornhusks (see opposite), aluminum foil, or parchment may be substituted.
BUTTER	Use only unsalted butter in all recipes. This helps you control the amount of salt in the recipe.
CHILES	Chiles provide more than heat—use them for their flavor, which varies subtly among varieties. Chiles and chile powders are available in many supermarkets as well as Hispanic and specialty markets.
ANCHOS	are dried poblanos with a spicy raisin flavor. For ancho puree, soak 6 chiles in 8 cups of boiling water for 30 minutes, drain, and puree in a blender with 1 tablespoon minced garlic and 2 tablespoons chopped cilantro.
CHIPOTLES	are dried jalapeños with a fiery, smoky flavor. They are available canned. For chipotle puree, process the peppers along with their sauce in a blender or food processor.
HABANEROS	range from green to red. They have a lot of heat and a fruity flavor.
JALAPEÑOS	are about 3 inches long and are green or red, depending upon ripeness. They provide a lot of heat.
POBLANOS	look something like dark bell peppers and are my favorite. They give mild, immediate heat (although the occasional poblano is fiery) and fresh pepper flavor.

CHORIZO	A spicy pork sausage, used in paella and Bolo Salad. The Spanish version is dry; a Mexican type is moist.
CILANTRO	Also known as coriander, a green herb with a pungent aroma.
CORNHUSKS, DRIED	Must be soaked in water until softened, then are used to wrap tamales. Available at Hispanic markets, they protect, moisten, and flavor food and prevent overcooking.
FLOUR, SEASONED	To 1 cup of all-purpose flour add 1 tablespoon salt and 1 tablespoon freshly ground black pepper.
MANCHEGO CHEESE	A Spanish sheep's milk cheese that originated in the area of La Mancha. It is semifirm and full flavored.
MESCLUN	Yellow, red, green, and white baby greens for salads.
OLIVE OIL	I use pure olive oil for most recipes.
ORZO	Small oval pasta resembling rice.
PEPPER	Use freshly ground pepper in all recipes.
PLANTAIN	A fruit that resembles the banana but is starchy and is cooked and served as a vegetable or dessert. Green are unripe, yellow are medium ripe, and black are ripe and sweet.
SALT	I use coarse, kosher salt for all my cooking. Crush it between your fingers and sprinkle it over food so you can feel exactly how much salt you're putting in.
SIMPLE SYRUP	Equal parts of sugar and water, cooked together over low heat until clear, then boiled 1 minute. Use for sangria.
TORTILLA	A thin pancakelike bread made from either blue or yellow cornmeal, or wheat flour.

Methods

BLANCH AND SHOCK

Plunge food into rapidly boiling water until al dente, cool in ice water, and drain. Blanch greens like cilantro or spinach for about 20 seconds, shock, and gently squeeze out the water.

CARAMELIZE

Cook food like onions or shallots slowly in oil until soft and golden, drawing out the natural sugar.

CHIFFONADE

Cut into fine strips. To cut sage or basil into chiffonade, roll the leaves up and cut into ribbons.

DEGLAZE

Add stock, juice, wine, or water to a pot or pan after cooking food, bring it to a boil, and stir to release the browned bits of food from the bottom and incorporate them into the liquid.

REDUCE

Concentrate a liquid by cooking over high heat. Let it boil but don't let it go crazy and splash all over the stove—you want it to reduce *in* the pan.

ROAST

GARLIC

Cut off the bud end, rub the head of garlic with olive oil, and wrap in foil. Roast at 300° F. for 45 minutes, or until soft.

BELL AND POBLANO PEPPERS

Rub peppers with olive oil, place on a baking sheet, and roast at 350° F. for 25 minutes, until softened and charred. To seed and peel, remove from the oven and place in a brown paper bag for 5 minutes. Cut in half, remove the seeds and stems, and peel off the skin.

CORN

Remove most of the husk, leaving one layer to cover the corn, and remove the silk. Dip in water, place on a sheet pan, and roast at 350° F. for 45 minutes. One ear of corn will yield about $\frac{1}{2}$ cup kernels.

ROAST **NEW POTATOES**	Rub with olive oil, sprinkle with salt and pepper, and place on a sheet pan. Roast at 350° F. for 45 minutes, or until done.
PEARL ONIONS	Rub with olive oil, sprinkle with salt and pepper, and place on a sheet pan. Roast in a 350° F. oven for 45 minutes, or until done.
SHALLOTS	Rub with olive oil, sprinkle with salt and pepper, and place on a sheet pan. Roast at 350° F. for 45 minutes, or until done.
SWEAT	Cook vegetables in oil over medium-high heat without coloring.
TEMPER	When making a custard or sauce, add a little heated milk or cream to beaten eggs, then pour the eggs back into the milk and mix. This prevents the eggs from scrambling.
TOAST **ALMONDS**	Preheat the oven to 350° F. Spread on a sheet pan and toast about 6 minutes, turning the pan once for even toasting and watching carefully so the nuts do not burn.
CUMIN, FENNEL, AND CORIANDER SEEDS	Cook seeds in a heavy dry pan over low heat 2 to 3 minutes, tossing or stirring until fragrant. Watch carefully so they don't burn.
TRUSS	Before roasting a chicken or turkey, secure the wings and legs with string.

Stocks

MAKES 2 QUARTS

CHICKEN STOCK

2 quarts cold water
2 pounds chicken carcasses
2 medium celery stalks, coarsely chopped
2 medium carrots, coarsely chopped
1 medium onion, coarsely chopped
6 peppercorns
1 bay leaf
8 parsley sprigs

Combine all the ingredients in a large pot and bring to a boil over high heat, skimming any scum that rises. Reduce the heat to low and simmer, uncovered, 2 hours.

Strain through cheesecloth or a fine strainer and degrease.

MAKES 1 TO 2 QUARTS

FISH STOCK

3 pounds bones from any whitefish
2 medium celery stalks, leaves removed, coarsely chopped
2 medium white onions, coarsely chopped
½ cup black peppercorns
2 bay leaves
2 cups white wine
Water to cover

Combine all the ingredients in a large pot and bring to a boil over high heat. Reduce the heat to low and simmer, uncovered, 30 minutes. Strain and discard the solids.

LOBSTER STOCK

2 tablespoons pure olive oil
Chopped shells of 2 roasted or boiled lobsters
1 large onion, coarsely chopped
1 small carrot, coarsely chopped
½ medium celery stalk, chopped
6 cups water
1 cup white wine
1 medium fresh tomato, chopped, or ½ cup
  canned plum tomatoes
1 bay leaf

In a large saucepan over high heat, heat the oil until almost smoking and sauté the shells, onion, carrot, and celery 5 minutes, stirring. Add the water, wine, tomato, and bay leaf. Reduce the heat to medium, partly cover, and simmer 40 minutes.

Strain through cheesecloth or a fine strainer.

SHRIMP STOCK

2 tablespoons pure olive oil
3 cups shells and tails from raw shrimp
1 large onion, coarsely chopped
1 small carrot, coarsely chopped
½ medium celery stalk, coarsely chopped
6 cups water
1 cup white wine
1 medium fresh tomato, chopped, or ½ cup
  canned plum tomatoes
1 bay leaf

In a large saucepan over high heat, heat the oil until almost smoking and sauté the shrimp shells and tails, onion, carrot, and celery 5 minutes, stirring. Add the water, wine, tomato, and bay leaf. Reduce the heat to medium, partly cover, and simmer 40 minutes.

Strain through cheesecloth or a fine strainer.

Each of these stocks may be refrigerated for up to 2 days, or frozen.

Getting
it All
Toget

At my table, the emphasis is on easy hospitality and a happy cook. Why prepare a feast if serving it keeps you too busy to sit down and enjoy it along with everyone else? And why make the same dishes you've always made when Latin flavors can light up your parties? If your dinners have always followed the stuffy pattern of appetizer-soup-salad-entrée-dessert, the meals you put together my way will be a real change. I'm not about formality—when I offer a meal to friends, there are no rules. My table is like a large canvas displaying the colors, aromas, and flavors of many kinds of dishes, all set out together. Sitting around, talking, drinking, and enjoying themselves, people fill their own plates as the spirit moves them. Timing and pacing take care of themselves, and the cook can just chill out and drink some sangria. Contrast this with the traditional party, where the host shuttles from kitchen to dining room and back again, serving course after course in order, so that by the time he or she finally gets to sit down, the others have already finished eating!

My party dishes make for a fragrant and bold mix: the exotic aroma of curry wafts over steaming paella as it comes off the stovetop; the sharp scent of chile oil accompanies roasted mushrooms with goat cheese; a garlic and hot pepper bouquet rises from burnished grilled steaks; juicy roasted grouper wrapped in fragrant banana leaves sits next to some garlicky roasted shrimp— and everything is heaped into large bowls or arranged on oversized platters. Pitchers of fruity sangria are on the table to add sparkle. Only the desserts—tropical fruit ices, ice cream, caramel-colored flans, and fruit-filled cakes and tarts—are brought out later.

her

Even that most traditional of meals, Thanksgiving dinner, can be served all at once and the surprise is, it's more fun that way. Imagine that it's Thanksgiving day and you're happily watching the football game. The turkey, stuffing, potatoes, and vegetables all have been done ahead and are waiting to be reheated in some simmering chicken broth. The salad has been made and, of course, so have the desserts—lots of them. (Forget about low-calorie Thanksgivings.) Suddenly, everyone wants turkey—now! So you just reheat all these things that you've already cooked, put them on trays and platters, and set them out, all at the same time, on your holiday table. Then you can pretend you're a guest.

For Thanksgiving dinner and all your other meals as well, remember that even though everything is presented at once, it doesn't have to be prepared that way. Many elements and even complete dishes are easy to make ahead and refrigerate. Sauces, vinaigrettes, and relishes can be done early and taken out of the refrigerator before mealtime. Oven-to-table dishes can be mixed ahead—or even cooked ahead and reheated later. Salads can be combined early in the day. Of course, desserts can be made ahead.

A few planning strategies will make everything go smoothly.

■ Establish your order of preparation—what you will do first, second, third, and so on. When I look at any dish or group of dishes, this immediately becomes obvious to me, but it may not be so clear to the home cook. To simplify your planning, the dishes for each grouping below will be listed in order of their preparation. Really plan out your meal so that you can enjoy it with your guests—that's the lesson of this book.

■ Do as much as you can ahead of time: clean the salad greens, mix the vinaigrette, cut the mint into chiffonade, chop the cilantro, slice the mangoes, fry the plantain chips, clean and sear the fish, cook the squid.

■ Use your appliances fully. When you can, stick to one appliance for cooking and maximize its use. If your oven will be on, plan to bake or roast more than one dish. Or combine oven and stovetop dishes in one meal.

■ Set out bowls of sauce, relish, and vinaigrette near several dishes to combine with any of them.

■ Every dish you serve need not be hot or cooked. Cool platters are time- and labor-savers, and side dishes of olives and cheeses will round out your table.

Here are some dishes that combine especially well. In most cases, they will help you make the best use of a single appliance. The recipes in each group are listed in the order of their preparation (except for the desserts and accompaniments—which should be made ahead).

MENU 1:
COOL PLATTERS
TABLE
	Spicy Jumbo Lump Crabmeat and Black Bean Salad with
	      Roasted Red Pepper Sauce and Cilantro Oil
	Saffron Rice Salad with Sweet and Fiery Dressing
	Red and Yellow Gazpacho with Grilled Sea Scallops
	Carpaccio of Beef with Oregano Vinaigrette, Arugula,
	      and Manchego Cheese
	Toasted Almond Flan

MENU 2	**Honey-Rum Baked Black Beans** **Cabbage and Green Bean Salad** **Yellow Corn–Coated Softshell Crabs with** **Red Chile–Mustard Sauce** **Fresh Green Pea and Toasted Coriander Risotto** **Fresh Pineapple Ices**
MENU 3	**Sea Scallop Ceviche with Grilled Red Onion** **and Mango-Tortilla Salad** **Grilled Steak with Garlic and Hot Pepper Marinade** **Lemon-Thyme Rice** **Grilled Plantains with Spicy Brown Sugar Glaze** **Fresh Pineapple Ices**

MENU 4

Garlic and Oregano–Marinated Grilled Chicken with
    Grilled Pepper and Black Olive Relish
Grilled Zucchini with Romesco Sauce
Cilantro Rice
Squid, Fried Plantain, and Mango Salad with
    Fresh Mint
Caramelized Fig Tart

MENU 5

Pan-Roasted Rabbit with Crushed
    Blackberry–Ancho Sauce
Broccoli Rabe with Caramelized Shallots
Bolo Salad with Chorizo, Cabrales Blue Cheese,
    and Tomatoes
Charred Yellow Tomato Risotto
Catalan Custard with Dried Fruits

MENU 6

Oven-Roasted Wild Mushrooms with
    Goat Cheese and Chile Oil
Saffron-Tomato Rice
Oven-Roasted Pork Tenderloin with Black Olive
    Tapenade and Charred Yellow Pepper Sauce
Grouper Roasted in Banana Leaves with
    Orange-Pineapple Relish
Bolo Roasted Apple Cake with Sherry Custard Sauce

MENU 7

Oven-Braised Lamb Shanks with Toasted Orzo
Wild Mushroom Rice
Oven-Baked Eggplant and Manchego Cheese Salad
    with Fresh Oregano and Balsamic Glaze
Spicy and Sweet Rum Plantains
Pomegranate Granita

MENU 8

Oven-Roasted Wild Mushrooms with Goat Cheese
    and Chile Oil
Cilantro Rice
Oven-Baked Eggplant and Manchego Cheese Salad
    with Fresh Oregano and Balsamic Glaze
Oven-Roasted Baby Shrimp with Toasted Garlic Chips
Chocolate-Coconut Bread Pudding

MENU 9

Black Beans and Rice

Crispy Shrimp and Potato Croquettes with
  Yellow Pepper Relish

Lobster Pan Roast with Salsa Verde and
  Spicy Tomato Relish

Bolo Salad with Chorizo, Cabrales Blue Cheese,
  and Tomatoes

Bolo Roasted Apple Cake with Sherry Custard Sauce

MENU 10

Oven-Roasted Tomato, Garlic, and Bread Soup

Curried Shellfish and Chicken Paella

Sophie's Salad

Spicy and Sweet Rum Plantains

Toasted Almond Flan

MENU 11

Grilled Tuna with Shellfish Mole Sauce

Saffron-Tomato Rice

Grilled Squid and Vidalia Onion Salad with Roasted
  Tomatoes and Green Chile Vinaigrette

Grilled Plantains with Spicy Brown Sugar Glaze

Coffee Ice Cream with Cinnamon Buñuelos and
  Very Rich Chocolate Sauce

MENU 12

Lemon-Thyme Rice

Pan-Roasted Filet Mignon with Rum–Red Chile Sauce

Baby Clams Steamed in Green Onion Broth

Oven-Baked Eggplant and Manchego Cheese Salad
  with Fresh Oregano and Balsamic Glaze

Pomegranate Granita

**MENU 13:
THANKSGIVING
DINNER**

Roasted Turkey with Pomegranate Sauce and
  Wild Rice and Goat Cheese Stuffing

Green Onion Smashed Potatoes

Broccoli Rabe with Caramelized Shallots

Wild Mushroom and Mizuna Salad with White
  Truffle Vinaigrette and Sage

Pumpkin Flan

Coffee Ice Cream with Cinnamon Buñuelos and
  Very Rich Chocolate Sauce

Bolo Roasted Apple Cake with Sherry Custard Sauce

From the Oven

Roasting, baking, and oven braising are all great techniques for my kind of informal entertaining. They produce dishes that are festive and hearty and they give the chef the bonus of fairly easy cleanups. If you use some nice-looking ovenproof earthenware, you can even cook and serve food in the same dish—just put it in the oven, take it out, and bring it to the table. You won't have to rearrange the food on a platter or wash extra dishes. The ingredients, juices, and flavors stay in the container so you don't lose anything in a transfer. And while the food is in the oven, you can use the stovetop to cook a versatile rice dish, sweet or savory tamales, or fresh vegetables.

Oven cooking simplifies entertaining, but that doesn't mean the food won't be complex and delicious. Oven-Roasted Baby Shrimp with Toasted Garlic Chips, Oven-Roasted Wild Mushrooms with Goat Cheese and Chile Oil, Honey-Rum Baked Black Beans, and Oven-Braised Lamb Shanks with Toasted Orzo are perfect examples of simple-to-make showcase dishes. And helping themselves to crusty, juicy, fragrant food from a steaming cazuela is fun for your guests, even if it can get a little competitive. When you add the extra steps of carving and arranging roasted chicken, turkey, or pork tenderloin on serving platters, your work won't increase by much and you will still present impressive food.

Prioritize! That's my first rule for entertaining, and I like the fact that it's easy to prep any of these dishes for cooking and then refrigerate them until party time. For example, when you make Roasted Chicken with Roasted Garlic Sauce and White Truffle Oil, you can do the sauce and marinade ahead of time and refrigerate the chicken in its marinade for 2 hours, or even overnight. Then you take the chicken out for about 10 minutes before you are ready to start

cooking, truss it, and put in the oven, and you're rolling. And several dishes can share oven space, so wild rice stuffing can cook along with turkey or wild mushrooms can roast next to grouper wrapped in banana leaves.

There is a difference between baking and roasting. Both happen in the oven, but baked food is covered and cooked at a lower temperature, making it the method of choice for juicy combinations or foods in a sauce. Roasting is best for tender cuts of meat and for poultry and vegetables. It sears in juices with dry heat (as opposed to direct heat on the stovetop), and the searing and cooking often are done in the same pan.

I like to roast with very high heat, at least at the beginning, to maximize the contrast between a crisp crust and a juicy interior. Start cooking chicken at 400° F., then turn down the heat, and it will be moist inside and crisp outside; if you cook it at 350° F. the whole time, it will be all one note. I use high heat for everything, including vegetables (except for slow-roasted garlic and tomatoes), so I can do several dishes in the oven at the same time. If the dishes lined up in my oven call for different temperatures, I can be somewhat flexible about the heat, remembering that if I raise it, cooking will be quicker and if I lower it, I must allow a bit more time.

Poultry or meat is always more flavorful and juicy roasted on the bone than cooked in pieces and a whole fish can be incredibly sweet and moist. Roasting on the bone just takes a bit longer, but eight small striped bass take only 12 to 14 minutes of oven time —and that's nothing!

Tougher cuts of meat take well to oven braising, which is low-heat cooking in liquid. First sear the food, then pour in a flavorful liquid like stock so that the cooking juices will run into the stock and the flavors will meld. Cook at about 300° F. and keep the pan covered so the juices don't evaporate before the meat is fully cooked.

Roasted Chicken with Roasted Garlic Sauce and White Truffle Oil

Why roast chicken the ordinary way when you can infuse it with subtle aromas and flavors? After its marination in olive oil with lots of garlic and herbs and its stint in a hot oven, this chicken comes out crisp-skinned and aromatic, with a great herbal flavor. The underlying note of garlic is repeated in a sweet roasted garlic sauce and the final touch of white truffle oil perfumes the finished dish.

FOR THE ROASTED GARLIC SAUCE

1 teaspoon butter
1 teaspoon pure olive oil
2 shallots, roughly chopped
1 cup port wine
8 cups Chicken Stock (page 46); do *not* substitute canned broth
2 heads of roasted garlic (page 44)
Salt

In a large sauté pan, heat the butter and olive oil over high heat until almost smoking and sauté the shallots until caramelized, about 3 minutes. Add the wine and reduce until almost dry. Add the stock and the roasted garlic and cook until reduced by half. Remove from the heat and strain into a saucepan.

Over medium-high heat, reduce until the sauce coats the back of a spoon, 5 to 7 minutes. Season to taste with salt and keep warm, or refrigerate up to 2 days and rewarm over low heat. Makes 3 cups.

FOR THE CHICKEN	2 cups pure olive oil
	⅓ cup finely chopped garlic
	⅓ cup roughly chopped fresh thyme leaves
	⅓ cup roughly chopped fresh tarragon
	⅓ cup roughly chopped fresh rosemary
	4 chickens, about 2½ pounds each
	Salt and pepper

Combine the olive oil, garlic, and herbs in a very large bowl. Stir well. Add the chickens and coat them with the marinade. Cover and refrigerate 2 hours or overnight.

Preheat the oven to 400° F. Truss the chickens (page 45) and season to taste with salt and pepper. Brush generously with the marinade.

Place in the oven and roast 10 minutes. Reduce the heat to 350° F. and continue roasting, basting regularly with the marinade and pan juices, until the chicken is cooked through and browned, about 30 minutes more. Remove from the oven and let rest.

TO SERVE	Roasted Garlic Sauce
	2 to 3 tablespoons white truffle oil (available at specialty stores and some supermarkets)

If necessary, reheat the roasted garlic sauce over low heat. Cut the chickens in half, arrange on a large platter, and drizzle with the truffle oil. Spoon the garlic sauce around the chicken.

Roasted Turkey with Pomegranate Sauce and Wild Rice and Goat Cheese Stuffing

MAKES 8 SERVINGS

With its dark, crisp skin and inviting herbal aroma, this turkey makes an awesome centerpiece for your holiday table. Serve it already sliced, so your guests can easily help themselves instead of sitting through the usual elaborate carving ritual while the rest of their food gets cold.

Preparing the turkey for roasting is simple: slip some fresh herbs under the skin, paint the top with a little melted butter, and sprinkle with salt and pepper. The key to a moist and tender bird is constant basting, so you should brush with the pan juices and melted butter every 10 minutes or so as it roasts. Start the cooking at high heat, about 450°F., then lower the heat after the skin gets nice and brown. If you have a small oven, cook the stuffing first and rewarm it later.

    1 fresh turkey, about 16 pounds
   20 fresh sage leaves (or fresh oregano)
    1 cup (2 sticks) butter, melted
       Salt and pepper
  1½ to 2 cups Pomegranate Sauce (page 213)
       Wild Rice and Goat Cheese Stuffing (page 164)

Preheat the oven to 450° F.

Remove the neck and gizzard from the turkey and discard. Rinse the bird thoroughly with cold water and pat dry. Using your fingers, gently loosen the skin from the breasts and drumsticks and slip the sage leaves underneath. Rub the entire surface with $\frac{1}{4}$ cup of the melted butter. Lightly sprinkle the skin and cavity with salt and pepper.

Truss the turkey and place on a rack in a large roasting pan. Roast for about 45 minutes, until brown, basting with the remaining butter every 10 minutes. Reduce the temperature to 350° F. and continue roasting for another $1\frac{1}{4}$ hours, or until an instant-read thermometer inserted in the thigh registers 180° F. If the legs or breast brown too quickly, cover them with foil.

Transfer the turkey to a cutting board and allow it to rest 20 to 30 minutes before carving.

To serve, cut down along each breast and remove it whole. Cut the breast into slices, the way you would slice a loaf of bread. Place on a large serving platter and arrange the thigh meat in chunks and the legs on top. Spoon some pomegranate sauce over the top and sprinkle everything with the pomegranate seeds and chives. Serve the remaining pomegranate sauce and the wild rice and goat cheese stuffing alongside.

You can reheat sliced turkey over medium heat in stock just to cover. Top with sauce, pomegranate seeds, and chives just before serving.

Oven-Braised Lamb Shanks with Toasted Orzo

MAKES 8 SERVINGS

Lamb shanks can be tough if they're not treated properly. But oven-cooked slowly in red wine with garlic and a lot of savory flavors, they will be tender and delicious.

Orzo, the pasta that looks like grains of rice, is normally just thrown into some boiling water like any ordinary pasta. But prepare it the way you would risotto, in the richly flavored stock that has infused the lamb shanks, and it will be incredible. Toasting it first in a dry pan adds a nutlike flavor, but brown only half the orzo, so the toasty note doesn't take over the dish. The idea was given to me by food writer Perla Meyers, who was born in Barcelona, where toasted orzo is traditional.

FOR THE LAMB SHANKS

8 lamb shanks, 1 to 1½ pounds each
Salt and pepper
¼ cup pure olive oil
1 medium Spanish onion, cut into large dice
1 large carrot, peeled and cut into large dice
1 large celery stalk, cut into large dice
2 heads roasted garlic (page 44)
2 cups port wine
2 cups red wine
4 fresh rosemary sprigs
4 fresh thyme sprigs
8 cups Chicken Stock (page 46) or canned low-sodium chicken broth
8 Oven-Roasted Tomatoes (page 126)

Preheat the oven to 300° F. Salt and pepper the lamb shanks liberally.

Heat the olive oil in a large sauté pan over high heat until smoking and sear the lamb shanks on all sides until dark brown.

Remove the shanks and pour off all but 2 tablespoons of the oil. Add the onion, carrot, and celery to the pan, lower the heat to medium-high, and cook until brown, about 5 minutes. Add the garlic and cook an additional 2 minutes. Add the port and red wine and reduce over high heat, scraping the pan, until almost dry.

Return the lamb shanks to the pan, add the rosemary and thyme, and pour in the stock. Cover and bring to a boil.

Place in the oven and bake until the meat is fork-tender, 2 to 2½ hours. Remove the meat to a platter or baking sheet. Strain the braising liquid and reserve 3 cups for the orzo.

Return the meat and remaining juices to the pan, place over high heat, and cook, turning the shanks often, until the liquid reduces and forms a glaze on the lamb shanks. Arrange the lamb shanks in a large shallow bowl and surround with the oven-roasted tomatoes.

FOR THE TOASTED ORZO

- ¼ cup (½ stick) butter
- 2 tablespoons pure olive oil
- 1 pound orzo
- 1 medium Spanish onion, finely diced
- 2 heads roasted garlic (page 44)
- 2 cups water
- 3 cups braising liquid reserved from the lamb
- ¼ cup chopped parsley
- Salt and pepper

Place a large sauté pan over medium-high heat and melt 2 tablespoons of the butter with the oil. Add half the orzo and cook, stirring constantly with a wooden spoon, until it turns a deep golden brown.

Add the onion and roasted garlic and cook, stirring, until the onion is transparent, about 1 minute.

Add the remaining orzo and stir. Add 1 cup water and cook until absorbed; repeat with the second cup of water.

Raise the heat to high and add the lamb braising liquid and the remaining butter. Cook until creamy (the mixture will thicken further when it is removed from the pan) and stir in the parsley. Season to taste with salt and pepper.

Oven-Roasted Pork Tenderloin with Black Olive Tapenade and Charred Yellow Pepper Sauce

MAKES 8 SERVINGS

Don't just throw this roast onto a serving dish—cut it into thick slices and arrange them on a bed of yellow pepper sauce to show off the juicy pork with its black olive center (see color pages).

FOR THE CHARRED YELLOW PEPPER SAUCE

2 yellow bell peppers, charred on the grill, seeded, and coarsely chopped (you can also char the peppers over a stove burner or under the broiler)

1/3 cup rice wine vinegar

6 roasted garlic cloves (page 44)

Pinch of saffron threads

1 tablespoon honey

1 teaspoon Dijon mustard

3/4 cup pure olive oil

Salt and pepper

In a blender or food processor, combine the peppers, vinegar, garlic, saffron, honey, and mustard and blend 30 seconds. With the motor running, slowly add the oil until it emulsifies. Season to taste with salt and pepper. Makes about 1½ cups.

FOR THE PORK TENDERLOIN

- 1 cup ancho chile powder (available at Hispanic or specialty markets)
- ½ cup paprika
- 1 tablespoon minced garlic
- ⅓ cup plus 3 tablespoons pure olive oil
- 2 pork tenderloins, 2 pounds each, butterflied
  Salt and pepper
  Black Olive Tapenade (page 220)
  Charred Yellow Pepper Sauce

Combine the ancho powder, paprika, garlic, and ⅓ cup of the olive oil in a mixing bowl and mix well. Set aside.

Preheat the oven to 400° F.

Season both sides of the pork tenderloins to taste with salt and pepper. Spread a thin layer of tapenade down the center, fold each side over the filling, and tie with butcher's twine. (If you have some tapenade left over, serve it on the side.) Coat with the reserved ancho mixture.

Heat the remaining 3 tablespoons of olive oil in a large sauté pan over medium to high heat until almost smoking and sear the pork on all sides. Place in a baking dish and roast until the outside is crusty and the meat is firm to the touch, about 10 minutes.

Let the tenderloin rest 10 minutes, then slice. Spoon the charred yellow pepper sauce onto a serving platter and top with the pork slices.

Spicy Maple-Glazed Pork Chops with Red Onion Marmalade and Blue Corn–Sweet Potato Tacos

Pork chops are a good foil for strong flavors because their meat is dense and somewhat tame. This glaze gives them spiciness from the chipotles and sweetness from the maple syrup. Red Onion Marmalade, served alongside, adds tart flavor as well as beautiful color. And together with Blue Corn–Sweet Potato Tacos—which are so blue that they are almost dark purple—this is a beautiful dish.

FOR THE SAUCE	8 cups Chicken Stock (page 46); do *not* substitute canned broth
	6 ounces frozen concentrated Granny Smith apple juice (available in supermarkets)
	¼ cup tightly packed dark brown sugar
	8 whole black peppercorns
	Salt

Combine the stock, apple juice, sugar, and peppercorns in a medium saucepan over high heat and reduce to 3 cups. Season to taste with salt and strain through a fine strainer. May be refrigerated up to 2 days. Makes 3 cups.

FOR THE MAPLE GLAZE	1½ cups maple syrup ¼ cup prepared horseradish, drained 2 tablespoons ancho chile powder (available at Hispanic or specialty markets)

In a small saucepan, combine the maple syrup and horseradish and bring to a boil over medium heat. Reduce the heat to low and simmer 10 minutes, stirring every 30 seconds.

Strain through a fine strainer, return to the saucepan, and add the ancho chile powder. Cook over low heat until thickened. Refrigerate up to 5 days; bring to room temperature before serving. Makes 1½ cups.

FOR THE PORK CHOPS	1 cup ancho chile powder (available at Hispanic or specialty markets) 1 cup pasilla chile powder (available at Hispanic or specialty markets) ½ cup finely chopped garlic (about 24 medium cloves) 1 center cut pork loin (9 bones) Salt and pepper 1½ cups Maple Glaze 3 cups sauce 3 cups Red Onion Marmalade (page 219) 8 Blue Corn–Sweet Potato Tacos (page 68)

Preheat the oven to 400° F.

In a small bowl, combine the chile powders and garlic. Season the pork loin to taste with salt and pepper and rub all surfaces with the chile mixture.

In a large roasting pan, roast the loin until medium rare, about 40 minutes. When cool enough to handle, cut between the bones into 8 chops.

In a heavy, ridged grill pan, sear the chops 3 minutes on each side, until grill marked. Place on a serving platter and brush with maple glaze. Serve with bowls of the sauce and the red onion marmalade. Accompany with a platter of blue corn–sweet potato tacos.

Blue Corn–Sweet Potato Tacos

MAKES 8 TACOS

Serve these with Spicy Maple-Glazed Pork Chops (page 66) and with any meat or poultry dish.

8 blue corn tortillas (available at Hispanic markets and some supermarkets)
2 cups grated white Cheddar cheese
2 cups grated Monterey Jack cheese
2 medium sweet potatoes, boiled, peeled, and cut into $\frac{1}{4}$-inch-thick slices
Salt and pepper
$\frac{1}{4}$ cup pure olive oil
1 tablespoon ancho chile powder (available at Hispanic or specialty markets)

Preheat the oven to 400° F.

Place 1 tortilla on a work surface. Cover half with $\frac{1}{4}$ cup of each cheese, top with 3 slices of sweet potato, and season to taste with salt and pepper. Fold the tortilla over to make a semicircle, brush the top with olive oil, and sprinkle with ancho chile powder. Repeat for the remaining tortillas. (At this point, they may be refrigerated several hours.) Place on a sheet pan and bake until crisp, about 6 minutes.

Oven-Roasted Baby Shrimp with Toasted Garlic Chips

MAKES 8 SERVINGS

You can find this classic Spanish dish in tapas bars in Spain and America. It is simply shrimp with garlic, oil, fresh thyme, and, in my version, a little chile. Roast it in an earthenware bowl and serve it right from the same dish, with some good bread to soak up the garlicky sauce. Toasted garlic chips make a great garnish: with each bite you get crisp texture and the taste of fresh garlic.

48	baby shrimp, shelled and deveined
½	cup Garlic Oil (page 211)
1½	tablespoons ancho chile powder (available at Hispanic or specialty markets)
2	tablespoons chopped fresh thyme
1	cup Toasted Garlic Chips (page 211)
	Salt and pepper

Preheat the oven to 500° F.

Place the shrimp in a bowl or ovenproof casserole, pour the garlic oil over them, and season with the ancho chile powder, salt and pepper. Roast until pink and cooked through, 6 to 7 minutes. Sprinkle with the chopped thyme and garnish with the garlic chips. Serve in the bowl.

Grouper Roasted in Banana Leaves with Orange-Pineapple Relish

MAKES 8 SERVINGS

Roasting fish wrapped in banana leaves is a Cuban kind of thing. The leaves keep the fish moist and at the same time impart a subtle banana flavor that is actually more herbaceous than fruity, almost musty—and very good. The technique is easy and is as appealing as the flavor. You can wrap the fish way ahead of time and refrigerate them on a sheet tray. Just throw them in the oven when you are ready to cook (see color pages).

> 8 grouper fillets, about 6 ounces each
> 6 tablespoons pure olive oil
>   Salt and pepper
> 2 banana leaves, each cut into 4 rectangles (available at Hispanic markets)
>   Chopped mint leaves, for garnish
>   Chopped cilantro leaves, for garnish
>   Diced red bell pepper, for garnish
>   Orange-Pineapple Relish (page 220)

Preheat the oven to 400° F. Rub each fillet with olive oil, season to taste with salt and pepper, and wrap envelope style in a banana leaf rectangle. Place seam-side down on a sheet pan and roast 8 to 10 minutes. When done, the fish will look a bit undercooked on top but will be firm and opaque.

Place the packets seam side up on a platter and fold back the sides of the banana leaf to expose the fish. Sprinkle with the mint, cilantro, and pepper. Serve the relish in a bowl alongside.

Roasted Monkfish with Salsa Verde

MAKES 8 SERVINGS

Herbaceous Salsa Verde is built on a base of tart tomatillos and adds a trio of fresh green herbs, along with garlic, wine, and clam juice. This forceful combination would knock out many lesser fish, but monkfish is strong and dense enough to stand up to it.

8 monkfish fillets, about 6 ounces each
3 tablespoons pure olive oil, plus extra for brushing the fish
Salt and pepper
Salsa Verde (page 217)

Preheat the oven to 400° F. Brush the monkfish lightly with oil and season to taste with salt and pepper.

In a large sauté pan, heat 3 tablespoons oil over high heat until almost smoking. Sear the monkfish until lightly browned, about 1 minute on each side. Transfer it to an ovenproof dish and roast in the oven to medium doneness, 6 to 8 minutes.

Place the fish on a serving plate and spoon the salsa verde over it.

Roasted Striped Bass with Red Pepper–Spanish Paprika Sauce

MAKES 8 SERVINGS

Paprika isn't just red powder, it's a basic spice in Spanish cuisine. To bring out its underlying flavor, toast it in a skillet and then use it in this deep red, vinaigrette-like sauce. The eight perfectly roasted fish, with deep magenta sauce ladled around them, make a strikingly beautiful platter.

This sauce can accompany other grilled whole fish or fillets.

FOR THE RED PEPPER–SPANISH PAPRIKA SAUCE

½ cup Spanish paprika
¼ cup red wine vinegar
1½ tablespoons honey
½ cup pure olive oil
5 red bell peppers, roasted, peeled, seeded, and coarsely chopped (page 44)
Salt and pepper

Toast the paprika in a large sauté pan over medium heat until the aroma emerges and the color deepens, about 2 minutes Be careful to keep the paprika moving all the time, either by shaking the pan or by stirring with a wooden spoon. Remove from the heat.

In a blender, combine the paprika with the vinegar and honey and blend well. Slowly add the olive oil and blend until emulsified. Add the bell peppers. Season to taste with the salt and pepper. Makes about 2 cups. May be refrigerated up to 2 days; bring to room temperature before serving.

8 **striped bass, 1 pound each, scaled and gutted**
¼ **cup pure olive oil**
 Salt and pepper
 Red Pepper–Spanish Paprika Sauce

Preheat the oven to 400° F. Make 4 diagonal cuts on each side of each fish, reaching all the way down to the bone. Brush each fish with oil and season to taste with salt and pepper.

Roast 12 to 14 minutes without turning, depending on the size and density of the fish.

Arrange the fish on a large serving platter and ladle the sauce over them.

Oven-Roasted Wild Mushrooms with Goat Cheese and Chile Oil

MAKES 8 SERVINGS

Wild mushrooms in a cazuela, Latin style, make one of our most popular appetizers at Bolo. They go straight from the oven to the table, and surprise you with contrasting flavors and textures (see color pages).

> 8 cups thinly sliced mushroom caps (a combination of portobello, shiitake, and oyster), about 2 pounds
> 3 tablespoons pure olive oil
> 3 garlic cloves, minced
> ¼ cup very finely sliced shallots
>   Salt and pepper
> 8 ounces goat cheese, cut into 8 slices
> 1 cup Chile Oil (page 210)
> 3 tablespoons fresh thyme leaves

Preheat the oven to 425° F.

In a large bowl, combine the mushrooms, olive oil, garlic, and shallots and season to taste with salt and pepper. Arrange evenly in one layer in a large, heavy roasting pan and roast until tender, about 15 minutes. Remove from the pan and cool at room temperature.

When ready to serve, preheat the oven to 425° F. Place the mushrooms in a large baking dish or casserole, drizzle with ½ cup chile oil, and top with the slices of cheese. Bake until hot, 5 to 8 minutes. Remove from the oven, garnish with thyme, and drizzle with the remaining chile oil. Serve hot.

Green Onion Smashed Potatoes

MAKES 8 SERVINGS

I was looking for something more exciting than just plain mashed potatoes, something with real texture, when I came up with this great combination. Be sure to smash the baked new potatoes while they are still very hot, as soon as they come out of the oven. Use a good heavy potato masher that will open them up, but don't let them get pureed and gluey. Add chopped scallions, roasted garlic, and softened butter (potatoes need *butter) for fantastic flavor and aroma.*

12	scallions
6	tablespoons pure olive oil
	Salt and pepper
16	new potatoes, quartered
1	head roasted garlic (page 44)
½	cup (1 stick) butter, softened

Preheat the oven to 450° F. Brush the scallions with 2 tablespoons of the oil and sprinkle with salt and pepper. Place on a sheet pan and roast 10 minutes. Remove from the oven and chop coarsely.

Toss the potatoes with the remaining olive oil and sprinkle with salt and pepper. Roast until just a bit overcooked but not brown or dry, about 25 minutes.

As soon as they come out of the oven, place the potatoes in a large mixing bowl and add the garlic, scallions, and butter. Smash vigorously with a potato masher to achieve a rustic texture—the mixture should not be smooth. Season to taste with salt and pepper.

To keep the smashed potatoes warm, put them in a bowl or pan, cover, and place the bowl in a larger pan of warm water.

Honey-Rum Baked Black Beans

MAKES 8 SERVINGS

Here is one of my favorite combinations—the sweetness of honey and the kick of rum go incredibly well with black beans. This is a great starch dish and a smooth, full-flavored backdrop for a crisp roasted whole fish (see color pages).

> 1 **pound dried black beans, picked over (or substitute 5½ cups drained canned black beans)**
> ½ **pound chorizo sausage, coarsely diced**
> 1 **small Spanish onion, diced fine**
> 2 **tablespoons minced garlic**
> 1 **medium carrot, peeled and diced fine**
> 1 **cup dark rum**
> ¼ **cup honey**
> **Salt and pepper**
> 3 **cups Chicken Stock (page 46) or canned low-sodium chicken broth**
> ¼ **cup coarsely chopped cilantro**

If using dried beans, place in a large pot with cold water to cover and let stand for 8 hours or overnight. Drain the beans and again add cold water to cover. Bring to a boil over high heat; then reduce the heat to medium and simmer until tender, about 1 hour. Drain and reserve.

Preheat the oven to 300°F.

In a sauté pan over medium-high heat, sauté the chorizo until it is brown and the fat is rendered, about 5 minutes. Remove the chorizo from the pan and pour off all but 3 tablespoons of the fat. Add the onion, garlic, and carrot and sweat until the onion is translucent and tender, about 4 minutes.

In a mixing bowl, combine the chorizo mixture with the beans, rum, and honey and season to taste with salt and pepper. Pour the mixture into a casserole or baking dish, add the stock, and cover.

Bake the beans 20 minutes. Check to see if the mixture is dry and add water or stock if needed. Continue baking, covered, another 25 minutes. Uncover and bake an additional 15 minutes. Remove from the oven and fold in the cilantro. Serve immediately.

om

Grill

Grilling is more than just a way to cook—it's a social experience built around food. When you fire up the grill and your guests gather round, get ready for a party within a party. Everybody will jump into the action, putting the steaks or fish on the fire, arranging the plates, setting the table, or just cruising with drink in hand and giving directions. Each person wants to have a part in the experience, even if it's only a small part. This is the most festive way to cook, and for the host, it's the most relaxed.

Grilled food should be served immediately—that's part of the fun. But it makes foods cooked over an open fire a little more

tricky than do-aheads like cool platters, roasts, or braised meats. Nevertheless, when you fill your table with grilled dishes, the marinades, sauces, and accompaniments can all be prepared well before cooking time. The game plan is, when your guests arrive, set out all the dishes you have done ahead to come to room temperature or be reheated. Then grill the main courses and put everything on the table. You'll have a lot of help!

For example, when you are planning to serve Grilled Tuna Marinated in Romesco Flavors with Melted Leeks and Onions and Oven-Dried Tomato Oil, make the sauce and the oil before your guests arrive. Ahead of time as well, sauté the leeks and onions with a little sugar, cook them down with fish stock and butter, and add some fresh thyme and capers. When your party is ready to begin, bathe the fillet in romesco sauce and grill it. Then you can put everything together instantly for an awesome dish.

In addition to following the specific recipes in this chapter, you can grill just about any kind of food, marinating it first, or simply brushing it with oil and sprinkling on some salt and pepper. Here are some general grilling times to help you plan:

STEAK: 4 MINUTES ON EACH SIDE FOR MEDIUM RARE

CHICKEN BREASTS: 4 MINUTES ON EACH SIDE

TUNA (6-OUNCE STEAKS): 2 MINUTES ON EACH SIDE

HALIBUT (6-OUNCE STEAKS): 3 MINUTES ON EACH SIDE

SWORDFISH (6-OUNCE STEAKS): 4 MINUTES ON EACH SIDE

MAKO SHARK (6-OUNCE STEAKS): 3 MINUTES ON EACH SIDE

SALMON (6-OUNCE STEAKS): 4 MINUTES ON EACH SIDE

SHRIMP, LARGE SEA SCALLOPS: 2½ MINUTES ON EACH SIDE

Vegetables are naturals for the grill—just brush them with olive oil and sprinkle with a little salt and pepper. Then throw them on and let them sizzle until tender, about 3 minutes on each side. It's important to have all vegetables the same thickness so they will cook evenly. Eggplant, zucchini, and yellow squash are best sliced ½ inch thick on the bias; bell peppers can be halved, stemmed, and seeded. Dense vegetables need some precooking so they won't burn before they are cooked through, so before grilling, boil potatoes and then slice them, and blanch broccoli and divide it into florets.

When the grill is hot you even can toss on thick slices of French bread brushed with olive oil. Toast them for about 1 minute on each side until crisp and spread with some creamy goat cheese.

My preference for a gas grill rather than charcoal is pretty well known. A gas grill heats up immediately and does a consistently good job of cooking. You just preheat it for 15 minutes, leaving it closed until you are ready to begin.

What can you do in the dead of winter? Grill outdoors and bring the food inside, or use a ridged grill pan on top of the stove, or use your broiler for close to the same results—but a little less fun.

Grilled Steak with Garlic and Hot Pepper Marinade

Grilled steak flavored with a marinade of fresh garlic, hot peppers, and sweet bell peppers is one of the ultimate steak dishes. The meat looks beautiful sliced, with its crisp crust and juicy pink center. But remember that this should marinate for 2 days (see color pages).

FOR THE GARLIC AND HOT PEPPER MARINADE

3 cups pure olive oil
1 head garlic clove, smashed
1 red bell pepper, roasted, quartered, peeled, and seeded (page 44), coarsely chopped
1 yellow bell pepper, roasted, quartered, peeled, and seeded (page 44), coarsely chopped
1 poblano pepper, roasted, quartered, peeled, and seeded (page 44), coarsely chopped
1 bunch of parsley
4 whole New Mexico red chiles, coarsely chopped
4 whole ancho chiles, coarsely chopped

Combine all the ingredients in a mixing bowl. May be refrigerated up to 1 day before using. Makes about 4 cups.

8 New York strip steaks, 10 ounces each
Garlic and Hot Pepper Marinade
Salt and pepper

Place the steaks in a shallow bowl and cover with ¾ of the marinade (refrigerate the remainder). Let marinate, refrigerated, 2 days, turning once after the first day.

Prepare a grill or preheat the broiler. Bring the extra marinade to room temperature.

Remove excess marinade from the steaks and season them on both sides to taste with salt and pepper. Grill or broil to your liking, or about 4 minutes on each side for medium rare. Slice the steaks and place on a large serving platter. Spoon the remaining marinade around the steaks.

Marinated Grilled Pork Tenderloin with Spicy Orange Vinaigrette

Despite its versatility, pork doesn't have a whole bunch of flavor. This marinade of chiles, garlic, and lime juice takes care of that, and grilling caramelizes the outside, creating a beautiful crust and a contrast of textures. The strong citrus flavor of orange vinaigrette echoes the tartness of the marinade.

FOR THE RED CHILE MARINADE

- ½ cup fresh lime juice
- ½ cup ancho chile powder (available at Hispanic or specialty markets)
- ½ cup pasilla chile powder (available at Hispanic or specialty markets)
- 2 teaspoons cayenne
- 1 cup pure olive oil
- 2 teaspoons each salt and pepper

In a food processor, combine the lime juice, chile powders, and cayenne and process 30 seconds. With the motor running, slowly add the olive oil and process until emulsified. Add the salt and pepper. May be refrigerated up to 1 day. Makes 2 cups.

5 **pounds pork tenderloin (about 8 pieces)**
Red Chile Marinade
Salt and pepper
Spicy Orange Vinaigrette (page 204)

Put the meat in a shallow bowl, pour in the marinade, cover, and refrigerate for 2 or up to 24 hours.

Prepare a grill or preheat the broiler.

Remove the meat from the marinade and season to taste with salt and pepper. Grill until medium, 10 to 12 minutes, turning and basting with the reserved marinade.

Slice into 2-inch pieces and arrange on a platter. Spoon the spicy orange vinaigrette alongside the pork.

Grilled Pork Chops with Charred Peppers and Onions and Caramelized Date Sauce

MAKES 8 SERVINGS

Everybody likes the combination of bell peppers and onions, especially with pork chops. In this classic Spanish preparation, the sweet, fruity date sauce plays off the savory flavors of the peppers and onions and provides balance to the dish.

FOR THE CARAMELIZED DATE SAUCE

1 tablespoon butter
1 cup thinly sliced shallots
2 tablespoons sugar
 Salt and pepper
2 cups port wine
2 cups coarsely chopped dates
8 cups Chicken Stock (page 46); do *not* substitute canned broth

Melt the butter in a large saucepan over medium heat. Add the shallots and the sugar and cook until caramelized, about 5 minutes. Season to taste with salt and pepper.

Increase the heat to medium-high. Add the port and let the mixture reduce to about $\frac{1}{2}$ cup. Add the chopped dates and stock and cook until the mixture reduces to about 2 cups and reaches the consistency of a slightly thick sauce, about 1 hour.

Reseason, then strain and keep warm over low heat. May be refrigerated up to 2 days and rewarmed over low heat. Makes 2 cups.

FOR THE PEPPERS AND ONIONS AND GRILLED PORK CHOPS

- **2 medium onions, sliced thin (don't separate into rings)**
- **5 tablespoons pure olive oil**
- **Salt and pepper**
- **4 red bell peppers**
- **4 yellow bell peppers**
- **8 pork chops, about 5 ounces each**

Prepare a grill or preheat the broiler.

Rub the onions with 1 tablespoon of the oil, sprinkle with salt and pepper, and grill 3 minutes on each side. Rub the peppers with 2 tablespoons oil and grill on all sides until the skin blisters and wrinkles. Peel off the skin, halve the peppers, and remove the seeds and stems. Cut into julienne strips and sprinkle with salt and pepper.

Brush the chops on both sides with the remaining oil and season to taste with salt and pepper. Grill or broil until medium, 5 minutes on each side.

Arrange the chops on a large serving platter and cover with the grilled onions and peppers. Spoon the sauce over all.

Skewered Lamb with Rioja Red Wine Vinaigrette

MAKES 8 SERVINGS

Marinating cubes of meat, threading them on skewers, and then grilling them over an open fire is a very Spanish thing to do. Since marination breaks down meat's connecting fibers, it always has been a good way to prepare tougher cuts for cooking, but I prefer to start with tender meat and use the aromatic bath of olive oil and herbs mainly to impart flavor. That way, marinating becomes a short process, the flavors are fresh, and the meat has perfect texture (see color pages). Serve with Tarragon Cracked Wheat Salad (page 175).

> 2 heads of garlic, cloves crushed
> 1½ cups pure olive oil
> 4 rosemary sprigs
> 8 lamb loins, about 5 pounds in all, cut into 3 ½-inch cubes
> 32 roasted pearl onions (page 45)
> 1½ cups Rioja Red Wine Vinaigrette (page 202)

Soak 8 bamboo skewers 6 inches long in water for 2 hours or overnight. (They should be waterlogged so they won't burn.)

In a large bowl, combine the garlic, olive oil, and rosemary and marinate the lamb 4 to 6 hours in the refrigerator.

Prepare a grill or preheat the broiler.

Thread the lamb cubes and roasted onions on the skewers and grill until rare to medium rare, about 3 minutes on each side. Place the lamb skewers on a serving platter and drizzle the Rioja vinaigrette over them.

Barbecued Baby Chicken with Mesa Barbecue Sauce and Wild Mushroom–Roasted Corn Relish

MAKES 8 SERVINGS

Tender chicken is infused with sweet and spicy flavors when it is brushed with Mesa Barbecue Sauce, which also gives it a delicious crust when grilled. A relish of crisp sweet corn and chewy mushrooms accents the juicy meat. With these baby birds, each person gets to eat a whole, perfectly flavored chicken.

FOR THE BARBECUED CHICKEN

8 baby chickens, about ¾ pound each
Mesa Barbecue Sauce (page 216)
Salt and pepper
Wild Mushroom–Roasted Corn Relish (page 225)

Prepare a grill or preheat the oven to 450°F.

Brush each chicken liberally with the barbecue sauce and season to taste with salt and pepper. Cook on the grill or in the oven until done, 15 to 20 minutes, basting continually with the sauce.

To serve, arrange the chickens on a large platter and spoon the relish over and around them.

Garlic and Oregano–Marinated Grilled Chicken with Grilled Pepper and Black Olive Relish

Marinate this chicken with tons of garlic and lots of fresh oregano (fresh is really the best, but if you can't find it, dried is acceptable). Then grill it like any ordinary chicken. The result will be far from ordinary—it will be full of great flavor (see color pages).

FOR THE GARLIC AND FRESH OREGANO MARINADE

- **2 tablespoons sherry vinegar (I prefer Spanish)**
- **2 tablespoons fresh lemon juice**
- **2 tablespoons fresh lime juice**
- **2 tablespoons honey**
- **1 tablespoon ancho chile powder (available at Hispanic or specialty markets)**
- **12 garlic cloves, coarsely chopped**
- **½ cup fresh oregano leaves**
- **2 cups pure olive oil**
- **Salt and pepper**

In a blender, combine the vinegar, lemon juice, lime juice, honey, ancho chile powder, garlic, and oregano and blend 30 seconds. With the motor running, slowly add the olive oil until emulsified. Season to taste with salt and pepper. Makes about 3 cups.

FOR THE CHICKEN	4 chickens, 2½ pounds each, cut into quarters
	Salt and pepper
	Garlic and Fresh Oregano Marinade
	Grilled Pepper and Black Olive Relish (page 221)

Season the chicken quarters with salt and pepper to taste and marinate in the garlic and fresh oregano marinade 2 hours, refrigerated.

Prepare a grill.

Remove the chicken quarters from the marinade and shake off any excess. Grill until done, about 10 minutes on each side, and place on a serving platter, surrounded by the relish.

Grilled Tuna with Shellfish Mole Sauce

MAKES 8 SERVINGS

A classic Mexican mole sauce is a combination of onions, chiles, and bitter chocolate usually served with chicken to make what lots of people consider the Mexican national dish, Mole Poblano. I expand the flavors by including saffron, roasted garlic, thyme, and cinnamon. And I build this delicious sauce on a foundation of Lobster Stock, which makes it a fantastic match for grilled tuna.

FOR THE MOLE SAUCE

¼	cup pure olive oil
4	yellow corn tortillas
2	ancho chiles, seeded and stemmed
2	New Mexico chiles, seeded and stemmed
1	pasilla chile, seeded and stemmed
½	medium red onion, coarsely chopped
½	head of garlic, roasted (page 44), cloves separated
½	cup slivered raw almonds
4	cups Lobster Stock (page 47), no substitutions
4	medium tomatoes, peeled, cored, and chopped
¼	cup golden raisins
½	ounce Mexican chocolate, chopped (Ibarra brand is available at Hispanic markets), or semisweet chocolate
2	tablespoons maple syrup
¾	teaspoon ground cinnamon
⅛	teaspoon ground cloves
	Juice of 1 lime
	Salt and pepper

In a large frying pan over medium heat, heat the oil to 375° F., or until a small bread cube sizzles on contact. Fry the tortillas and all the chiles until crisp, 10 to 15 seconds. Remove with tongs and place in a food processor or blender. Add the onion and garlic to the oil and fry until browned, about 2 minutes; add to the processor. Pour out all but 2 tablespoons of the oil and toast the almonds until golden brown. Add to the processor.

Add 1 cup of stock to the processor and process the tortillas, chiles, onion, garlic, and almonds to a puree, adding more stock if needed.

Pour the puree into a medium saucepan and add the remaining stock, the tomatoes, and raisins. Bring to a boil over medium-high heat; reduce the heat to medium and simmer 1 hour and 20 minutes, stirring frequently.

Add the chocolate, maple syrup, cinnamon, cloves, and lime juice. Season to taste with salt and pepper and simmer another 15 minutes. Remove from the heat. May be refrigerated up to 2 days or frozen; reheat before serving. Makes 5 cups.

FOR THE GRILLED TUNA

8 tuna steaks, each 1½ to 2 inches thick, about 6 ounces
Pure olive oil
Salt and pepper
Mole Sauce

Prepare a grill or preheat the broiler.

Brush the tuna steaks with the oil and season to taste with salt and pepper. Grill or broil 2 minutes on each side for rare, or to taste. Place on a large serving platter and spoon the mole sauce over and around them.

Grilled Salmon with Sherry Vinegar–Honey Glaze and Spicy Tomato Relish

MAKES 8 SERVINGS

The flavors of Spain inspired this beautifully simple fish dish. For the best results, it is important to use really good-quality aged sherry vinegar.

Excellent farm-raised salmon, with consistent flavor and texture, is easy to find at local fish markets. I prefer it to wild salmon.

1	cup sherry vinegar (I prefer aged Spanish)
1/4	cup Dijon mustard
1/2	cup honey
2	tablespoons ancho chile powder (available at Hispanic or specialty markets)
	Salt and pepper
8	salmon fillets, 5 to 6 ounces each
	Spicy Tomato Relish (page 222)

In a small saucepan over high heat, reduce the vinegar to about $\frac{1}{4}$ cup of syrup. In a mixing bowl, combine the vinegar syrup with the mustard, honey, and ancho chile powder and season to taste with salt and pepper. Let rest at room temperature 30 minutes.

Prepare a grill or preheat the broiler.

Brush the salmon with the glaze and grill 3 minutes on each side for medium.

Arrange on a large platter and surround with relish.

Grilled Salmon Brushed with Black Olive Vinaigrette

MAKES 8 SERVINGS

Black Olive Vinaigrette adds contrasting savory flavors to rich salmon fillets—just brush the fish with the vinaigrette as it grills. If you like, serve some aromatic Saffron-Tomato Rice (page 145) alongside.

**8 salmon fillets, 6 ounces each
Black Olive Vinaigrette (page 200)
Salt and pepper**

Prepare a grill or preheat the broiler.

Brush the salmon fillets with the vinaigrette and season to taste with salt and pepper. Grill until medium, 4 minutes on each side, basting several times with more of the vinaigrette.

Place the fillets on a serving platter and serve the remaining vinaigrette on the side.

Grilled Snapper in White Bean and Chickpea Broth with Roasted Garlic Aioli

MAKES 8 SERVINGS

The great thing about this dish is you can make the broth and the roasted garlic aioli ahead of time and then grill the snapper when you are ready to put it all on the table. Serve the fish in the broth and the aioli on the side. Tell your guests to take some aioli and stir it into their broth—that way they can add as much garlic to the dish as they want.

FOR THE ROASTED GARLIC AIOLI	**1 cup roasted garlic cloves (page 44)** **1 cup good-quality mayonnaise** **Salt and pepper**

Peel the garlic and place the cloves in a food processor. Add the mayonnaise and process to a puree. Season to taste with salt and pepper. May be refrigerated up to 2 days; bring to room temperature before serving. Makes about 1¼ cups.

FOR THE WHITE BEAN AND CHICKPEA BROTH	**1** tablespoon pure olive oil **3** tablespoons finely chopped garlic **¼** cup white wine **4** cups Shrimp Stock (page 47) or clam juice **2** cups cooked chickpeas (or substitute canned) Salt and pepper **1** cup cooked white beans (or substitute canned) **2** tablespoons chopped fresh thyme

Heat the oil in a medium saucepan over medium heat and sauté the garlic until toasted. Add the wine, stock, and 1 cup of the chickpeas, raise the heat to high, and bring to a boil. Season with salt and pepper and puree in a food processor. Pour the mixture back into the saucepan.

Add the remaining chickpeas, the white beans, and thyme and cook 5 minutes over medium heat. Season to taste with salt and pepper. May be refrigerated up to 2 days; reheat over medium heat. Makes about 8 cups.

FOR THE SNAPPER	**8** snapper fillets, about 6 ounces each **2** tablespoons pure olive oil Salt and pepper White Bean and Chickpea Broth **8** thyme sprigs, for garnish Roasted Garlic Aioli

Prepare a grill or preheat the broiler.

Rub the fillets with olive oil and season to taste with salt and pepper. Grill or broil until lightly brown, about 4 minutes on each side.

Ladle the white bean and chickpea broth into a large, shallow bowl. Place the grilled fillets on top and garnish with the thyme sprigs. Serve the aioli on the side.

Grilled Tuna Marinated in Romesco Flavors with Melted Leeks and Onions and Oven-Dried Tomato Oil

MAKES 8 SERVINGS

The elements of a classic Spanish romesco sauce are combined here into a marinade for fresh tuna (the marinade is a little thinner than the sauce, which appears on page 102). Grilled tuna is piled onto a bed of savory melted leeks and onions and drizzled with a sweet and tangy tomato oil that echoes the tomatoes in the marinade. Accompany this rich and varied dish with your favorite rice (see color pages).

½ cup pure olive oil
¼ cup peeled garlic cloves
1 red bell pepper, roasted, peeled, and seeded (page 44)
2 plum tomatoes
2 ancho chiles, soaked in boiling water until soft, seeded
1 slice of white bread, crust removed, cut into small cubes
½ cup red wine vinegar
¼ cup red wine
¼ cup shelled hazelnuts
1 tablespoon honey
Salt and pepper

Heat the olive oil in a large sauté pan over high heat until smoking. *Separately* sauté the garlic, bell pepper, tomatoes, chiles, and bread cubes until lightly browned, about 2 minutes each. Remove each ingredient with a slotted spoon as it's done. Deglaze the pan with the vinegar and red wine (you can pour both in at the same time).

Place all the sautéed ingredients and the deglazing liquid into a food processor and blend until smooth. Add the hazelnuts and process until finely chopped. Add the honey and season to taste with salt and pepper. May be refrigerated up to 2 days. Makes about 3 cups.

FOR THE MELTED LEEKS AND ONIONS

4 tablespoons (½ stick) butter
2 medium white onions, sliced thin
4 large leeks, washed well and sliced ¼ inch thick (green and white parts)
8 garlic cloves, sliced thin
2 tablespoons sugar
2 cups clam juice
2 tablespoons small capers
2 tablespoons fresh thyme leaves
Salt and pepper

Melt the butter in a sauté pan over medium-high heat and sweat the onions, leeks, and garlic 5 minutes. Add the sugar and sauté the mixture 3 minutes. Add the clam juice, reduce the heat to low, and cook until very soft. Drain, and then fold in the capers and thyme. Season to taste with salt and pepper. May be refrigerated up to 2 days; reheat over low heat. Makes about 8 cups.

FOR THE TUNA	**8 tuna steaks, 5 to 6 ounces each** **Salt and pepper** **Romesco Marinade** **Melted Leeks and Onions** **Oven-Dried Tomato Oil (page 212)**

Prepare a grill or preheat the broiler.

Season the tuna with salt and pepper to taste and marinate for 5 minutes in the romesco marinade. Grill 2 minutes on each side; the tuna should be rare.

To serve, make a layer of melted leeks and onions on a serving platter, top with the fillets, and drizzle the tomato oil over and around.

Grilled Plantains with Spicy Brown Sugar Glaze

MAKES 8 SERVINGS

I love this dish, especially with savory fish, grilled outdoors. Ripe plantains have great texture—they are still a little bit firm, but kind of soft inside. Because they have their own natural sugars, they have a great affinity for sweet flavors like this brown sugar glaze. Obviously, the main influence here is Cuban, but grilling, rather than the more traditional methods of baking or frying, makes plantains almost a new food (see color pages).

> **6 very ripe plantains (they should be almost black), peeled and sliced on the bias ¼ inch thick**
> **1 tablespoon pure olive oil**
> **4 tablespoons light brown sugar**
> **1 tablespoon honey**
> **1 canned chipotle, pureed (about ½ tablespoon puree)**
> **2 tablespoons coarsely chopped cilantro**
> **Salt and pepper**

Prepare a grill.

Brush the plantains with olive oil and grill until caramelized, about 2 minutes on each side.

In a small bowl, combine the brown sugar, honey, chipotle puree, and cilantro and brush on the plantains. Season to taste with salt and pepper.

Grilled Zucchini with Romesco Sauce

This is my chile-spiked variation of romesco, a classic Spanish sauce based on tomatoes, garlic, olive oil, vinegar, and nuts. It is traditionally served with fish or meat—not vegetables—but I find it is a perfect match for grilled zucchini, giving that simple vegetable a real infusion of flavor and fire (see color pages).

FOR THE ROMESCO SAUCE

- ¼ cup pure olive oil
- ¼ cup peeled garlic cloves
- 1 red bell pepper, roasted, peeled, and seeded (page 44)
- 2 plum tomatoes
- 2 ancho chiles, soaked in boiling water until soft, seeded
- 1 slice of white bread, crust removed, cut into small cubes
- ¼ cup red wine vinegar
- ¼ cup red wine
- ¼ cup shelled hazelnuts
- 1 tablespoon honey
- Salt and pepper

Heat the olive oil in a large sauté pan over high heat until smoking. *Separately* sauté the garlic, bell pepper, tomatoes, chiles, and bread cubes until lightly browned, about 2 minutes each. Remove each ingredient with a slotted spoon as it's done. Deglaze the pan with the vinegar and red wine (you can pour both in at the same time).

Place all the sautéed ingredients and the deglazing liquid into a food processor and blend until smooth. Add the hazelnuts and process until finely chopped. Add the honey and season to taste with salt and pepper. Makes about 2½ cups.

FOR THE GRILLED ZUCCHINI	4 medium zucchini, cut on the bias into ¼-inch slices Romesco Sauce Salt and pepper

Prepare a grill.

Five minutes before grilling, marinate the zucchini slices in 1 cup of the romesco sauce.

Season the zucchini with salt and pepper to taste and grill until tender, about 2 minutes on each side. Place on a serving platter and serve the extra romesco sauce on the side.

From the Stovetop

Chefs rely on stovetop cooking even more than home cooks do. We turn the burners up high and sauté, toss, fry, steam, and stir vigorously so we can get the food out in a hurry and keep the customers happy. While you won't be working in that kind of frenzy at home, quick preparation can sometimes be important if you are pulling together several parts of a complex meal. That's when you can take full advantage of your stovetop.

Probably the most versatile kitchen appliance, the stove handles a full range of techniques (no pun intended) and turns out food with a variety of distinct tastes and textures. You can sauté fresh Broccoli Rabe with Caramelized Shallots; pan-roast lobster, rabbit, or filet mignon; and steam tamales or plantains. And you can fry crisp Shrimp and Potato Croquettes, squid, or Batter-Fried Potatoes.

Nothing beats its efficiency in last-minute cooking, either when you prepare a dish entirely on the stove, such as Baby Clams Steamed in Green Onion Broth, or just finish one whose elements have been cooked earlier, like a savory Latin soup made of oven-roasted tomatoes, garlic, and bread.

Your stovetop can produce an entire tableful of dishes or it can be an adjunct to your oven, broiler, or grill. If you are making Oven-Braised Lamb Shanks the center of your table, the stovetop provides the accompanying toasted orzo. While your oven roasts baby shrimp with fragrant garlic, herbs, and a touch of chile, the garlic chips that go along with it crisp on the stove. A simmered shellfish mole sauce is served over tuna prepared on the grill, and snapper hot from the grill is served in white bean and chickpea broth that has cooked gently on your range. (You can find these recipes in the appropriate chapters.)

Stovetop cooking is essential when you want to get a really nice sear on meat or fish and retain its juices, and it's especially good for things you have to be careful with—foods that require moderate heat and some vigilance. The range is at its absolute best when you want to coat fish or seafood in a snappy, flavorful crust, as with some of my favorite dishes: Potato and Cascabel–Crusted Halibut with Mango–Carrot Broth and Mango-Green Onion Salsa, Almond-Crusted Cod with Preserved Oranges and Spicy Orange Vinaigrette, Tapenade-Crusted Salmon, and Yellow Corn–Coated Softshell Crabs with Red Chile–Mustard Sauce. Only the stovetop can provide the even, direct heat you need to cook a crust to crispness while retaining the delicate texture of the food it encases. If you try this process on the grill or in the oven or broiler, you are likely to burn the herbs or nuts and dry out the fish or shellfish, ruining its texture. Texture is as important as taste, and using the stove burners is the surest way to monitor it as you cook.

Pan-Roasted Rabbit with Crushed Blackberry—Ancho Sauce

MAKES 8 SERVINGS

Rabbit is popular in all the Latin countries, perhaps because it is moister, denser, and more flavorful than chicken. This loin is stuffed with fresh spinach, rolled tightly, and seared in a pan on the stovetop to give it a golden-brown crust. Then it is roasted until cooked through. When the meat is cut into thick slices, each one reveals a bright green center. Serve a sweet and spicy blackberry sauce and green onion tamales alongside (see color pages).

½ cup all-purpose flour
3 tablespoons cascabel chile powder (available at Hispanic or specialty markets) or another hot chile powder
Salt and pepper
8 rabbit loins, about 6 ounces each, boned and butterflied
1 pound fresh spinach, washed and stems removed
¼ cup pure olive oil
Crushed Blackberry–Ancho Sauce (page 214)
Green Onion Tamales (page 130)

Preheat the oven to 450°F. In a mixing bowl, combine the flour and chile powder and season to taste with salt and pepper. Season the rabbit loins to taste with salt and pepper.

In a large pot of boiling salted water over high heat, blanch the spinach until wilted, about 30 seconds. Shock in a bowl of ice water and squeeze dry.

Divide the spinach among the rabbit loins, placing it in the center of each. Roll up the meat and tie with kitchen string. Dredge the rolls in the flour mixture and shake off the excess. In a large ovenproof sauté pan over medium-high heat, heat the oil until almost smoking and sear the rolls until slightly crusty, about 1 minute on each side.

Place the pan in the oven and cook the meat an additional 8 minutes for medium, or until done to taste. Let rest at room temperature about 2 minutes.

To serve, slice each roll into medallions and arrange on a large serving platter. Accompany with crushed blackberry-ancho sauce and green onion tamales.

Pan-Roasted Filet Mignon with Rum–Red Chile Sauce

MAKES 8 SERVINGS

While filet mignon is nice and tender, the flavor isn't always there. This cut of meat needs an extra kick, and the rum and red chiles—inspired by Cuba and Mexico—provide that very well. First I sear these steaks in a pan and then I put them in the oven to cook through. You can grill them instead, if you prefer.

FOR THE RUM–RED CHILE SAUCE

- **2 tablespoons (¼ stick) butter**
- **3 shallots, minced**
- **1 tablespoon minced garlic**
- **1 cup Myers's dark rum**
- **4 cups Chicken Stock (page 46); do *not* use canned**
- **2 tablespoons ancho puree (see page 42)**
- **2 tablespoons molasses**
- **Salt and pepper**

Melt the butter in a saucepan over medium-high heat and sweat the shallots and garlic. Add the rum, bring to a boil, and reduce to ⅓ cup.

Add the stock, bring to a boil, and reduce the heat. Whisk in the remaining ingredients and simmer until reduced to 2 cups. May be refrigerated up to 2 days; reheat with a little water and reseason.

8 **filet mignon steaks, about 8 ounces each**
Salt and pepper
2 **tablespoons (¼ stick) butter**
Rum–Red Chile Sauce

Preheat the oven to 450° F. and season the steaks to taste with salt and pepper. In an ovenproof skillet or sauté pan over medium heat, melt the butter and sear the steaks on one side about 3 minutes. Place in the oven and cook to the desired doneness.

Place the steaks on a serving platter and drizzle with the rum–red chile sauce. Serve any extra sauce on the side.

Potato and Cascabel–Crusted Halibut with Mango–Carrot Broth and Mango–Green Onion Salsa

MAKES 8 SERVINGS

Chefs, figuring out that the texture of food is as important as its flavor, have discovered the technique of crusting. But this is not just for chefs—it is easy enough to do at home. Here, crunchy shredded potatoes form a protective crust over silky halibut and cascabel chiles add an extra jolt of heat. Sweet mangoes flavor the broth that surrounds the fish and the relish that accompanies it (see color pages).

FOR THE MANGO-CARROT BROTH

2 cups fresh mango juice or canned mango nectar

2 cups fresh carrot juice, from about 8 carrots, or use purchased juice

1 tablespoon toasted whole fennel seeds (page 45)

2 tablespoons toasted whole coriander seeds (page 45)

1 habanero chile

Salt and pepper

In a medium saucepan over high heat, combine the juices, fennel, coriander, and chile and bring to a boil. Reduce the heat and simmer 20 minutes, or until reduced by half.

Strain through a fine strainer and season to taste with salt and pepper. Makes 2 cups. May be refrigerated up to 2 days; reheat over medium heat.

FOR THE POTATO AND CASCABEL-CRUSTED HALIBUT

8 **halibut fillets, 5 to 6 ounces each**
Salt and pepper
2 **large Idaho potatoes, peeled and shredded**
4 **teaspoons cascabel chile powder (available at Hispanic or specialty markets) or another hot chile powder**
4 **tablespoons pure olive oil**
Mango-Carrot Broth
Mango–Green Onion Salsa (page 218)

Season the fillets on both sides to taste with salt and pepper. Cover the flesh side with a thin layer of the shredded potatoes, pressing down so it adheres, and sprinkle with the chile powder.

Heat the olive oil in a large sauté pan over medium-high heat until it begins to smoke. Cook the fillets, potato-side down, until the potatoes are lightly browned and cooked through, about 2 minutes. Reduce the heat to medium, turn the fillets, and cook until done to taste, an additional 3 to 4 minutes.

Pour the mango-carrot broth into a large serving bowl and arrange the fillets in the bowl. Top each fillet with mango–green onion salsa and serve any remaining salsa on the side.

Potato-Horseradish —Crusted Red Snapper with Roasted Pepper Relish

At Bolo, my Spanish restaurant in New York, we wrap red snapper in a crust of crisp potatoes and pungent horseradish. Horseradish is a great but generally underutilized flavor. It electrifies this dish and melds perfectly with the flavors in the Roasted Pepper Relish.

8 red snapper fillets, 5 to 6 ounces each
   Salt and pepper
1 large potato, peeled and finely grated
½ cup prepared horseradish, drained
4 tablespoons pure olive oil
   Roasted Pepper Relish (page 224)

Preheat the oven to 350° F.

Season each fillet to taste with salt and pepper. Combine the potato and horseradish and spread the mixture over the top of each fillet, pressing down so it will adhere.

Heat the oil in a large sauté pan over medium heat until almost smoking. Sear each fillet potato-side down until a crust forms, about 3 minutes. Turn the fillets over and finish cooking in the oven until done, about 5 minutes for medium. Place on a large serving platter and top each fillet with some relish. Serve any remaining relish on the side.

Tapenade-Crusted Salmon

The secret to cooking this salmon without burning its black olive coating is to brown the crust quickly and then turn over the fish and finish cooking the other side. Don't use too much tapenade—the bold flavors of olives, garlic, and anchovies can overpower the salmon.

8 salmon fillets, 6 ounces each
Salt and pepper
Black Olive Tapenade (page 220)
¼ cup pure olive oil
Flat-leaf parsley sprigs, for garnish

Season each fillet to taste with salt and pepper. Press the tapenade over the flesh of each fillet (not the skin side).

Heat the oil in a large sauté pan over high heat until it begins to smoke. Sear the fillets, tapenade-side down, until a crust forms, about 1½ minutes. Lower the heat to medium, turn the fillets, and cook until rare to medium, about 5 minutes.

Arrange the fish on a serving platter and garnish with the parsley sprigs.

Almond-Crusted Cod with Preserved Oranges and Spicy Orange Vinaigrette

MAKES 8 SERVINGS

With its classic combination of almonds and oranges, this dish hollers "Spain!" Coating cod with crushed almonds and serving it with a tangy orange vinaigrette enhances its mild flavor and superb texture.

FOR THE PRESERVED ORANGES	3 cups sugar
	3 cups water
	2 large oranges, unpeeled, sliced ⅛ inch thick

Bring the sugar and water to a simmer in a wide, 6-quart nonreactive saucepan over medium heat. Add the orange slices and simmer 10 minutes, until the oranges are softened, stirring occasionally so the slices don't stick together. Remove from the heat and let cool at room temperature 10 to 15 minutes.

Remove the oranges from the syrup, arrange in a single layer on a wire rack on a baking sheet lined with wax or parchment paper, and dry at room temperature for about 1 hour. May be refrigerated up to 3 days. Bring to room temperature before serving. Makes about 16 slices.

	4 large eggs, lightly beaten
	Salt and pepper
	2 cups seasoned flour (page 43)
FOR THE COD	2 cups finely crushed almonds
	8 cod fillets, about 6 ounces each
	½ cup pure olive oil
	Preserved Oranges
	Spicy Orange Vinaigrette (page 204)

Season the eggs lightly with salt and pepper. Place the eggs, flour, and almonds in 3 separate bowls. Season the fillets lightly on both sides with salt and pepper and dredge the flesh (not the skin side) in flour, shaking off the excess. Dip the floured side in the egg and let the excess drip off. Then dip into the crushed almonds to coat.

Heat the oil in a large sauté pan over medium heat until it begins to smoke. Sear each fillet on the coated side until the almonds turn light golden brown, about 3 minutes. Turn the fish over and cook until medium, another 3 to 4 minutes.

To serve, arrange on a large platter. Garnish with the preserved oranges and drizzle with the spicy orange vinaigrette.

Yellow Corn–Coated Softshell Crabs with Red Chile–Mustard Sauce

*Here is the heart of my favorite weekend lunch: an enormous platter
of cornmeal-crusted crabs accompanied by a bowl of crisp Cabbage
and Green Bean Salad (page 176), served outdoors—preferably next
to a swimming pool (see color pages).*

16	live softshell crabs
1	cup all-purpose flour
1	cup yellow cornmeal (coarse grind)
4	large eggs, lightly beaten
	Salt and pepper
½	cup pure olive oil
4	tablespoons (½ stick) butter
	Red Chile–Mustard Sauce (page 215)

Clean the soft-shell crabs: Cut off the mouth and eyes with scissors.
Lift up both sides of the shell and cut out the spongy gills. Cut off
the "apron" that is on the underside of the crab.

Place the flour, cornmeal, and eggs in separate bowls and season
each to taste with salt and pepper. Dredge each crab in flour, shake
off any excess, and dip into the beaten eggs, covering completely.
Dredge in the cornmeal.

Heat 2 tablespoons of the oil and 1 tablespoon of the butter in a large sauté pan over medium heat until it begins to smoke. Sauté 4 crabs at a time until crisp, 2 to 3 minutes on each side. Remove to a platter lined with paper towels. Wipe out the pan each time with a clean cloth or paper towel.

Arrange the crabs on a large serving platter. Accompany with red chile–mustard sauce.

Lobster Pan Roast with Salsa Verde and Spicy Tomato Relish

MAKES 8 SERVINGS

Pan-roasting is one of the easiest ways I know to cook lobster. And this recipe is great for entertaining—make the Salsa Verde and the Spicy Tomato Relish ahead of time, and you're home free.

- 8 live lobsters, about 1½ pounds each
- 4 tablespoons pure olive oil
  Salt and pepper
- 6 cups Salsa Verde (page 217)
- 16 new potatoes, roasted and halved (page 45)
  Spicy Tomato Relish (page 222)

Preheat the oven to 350° F.

To kill the lobsters, insert a sharp knife into the cross mark on the top shell between the head and the body. Pull or cut off the claws. Pull or cut off the tails and cut in half lengthwise. Discard the bodies.

Heat the olive oil in a large ovenproof sauté pan over medium-high heat until smoking. Season the lobster pieces to taste with salt and pepper and sear 3 minutes. Pour off any excess oil.

Add the salsa verde and potatoes to the pan and season to taste with salt and pepper. Place the pan in the oven and roast until the lobster is cooked through, 15 minutes. Reseason if necessary.

Arrange the lobsters on a large platter and spoon the relish over them.

Baby Clams Steamed in Green Onion Broth

Here, tiny clams are cooked and served in a light, very herbaceous, oniony broth, perfect for mopping up with thick slices of bread (see color pages).

6	tablespoons pure olive oil
2	tablespoons chopped garlic
1	medium onion, peeled and sliced thin
4	cups clam juice
2	cups white wine
6	tablespoons fresh lemon juice
2	cups tightly packed parsley leaves
2	tablespoons honey
	Salt and pepper
80	baby clams

Heat the oil in a large saucepan over medium-high heat until almost smoking and sauté the garlic until golden brown. Add the onion and cook until soft. Add the clam juice, wine, and lemon juice and bring to a boil. Reduce the heat and simmer 15 minutes. Remove from the heat and let cool to room temperature.

In a blender, combine the onion broth with the parsley, honey, and salt and pepper to taste and process until pureed.

Combine the clams and onion broth in a large saucepan over high heat and bring to a boil. Reduce the heat to medium, cover the pan, and steam the clams until opened, about 3 minutes after the broth begins to boil. Discard any that do not open.

Spoon the clams into a large bowl with the onion broth.

Crispy Shrimp and Potato Croquettes with Yellow Pepper Relish

MAKES 8 SERVINGS

Texture is what really attracts your attention in these Latin-inspired croquettes. Your fork breaks a crisp surface (provided by a rice flour batter) and exposes a creamy center filled with nuggets of potato and shrimp. Yellow pepper relish contributes further contrast as well as bright color.

FOR THE RICE FLOUR BATTER	1½ cups rice flour
	¾ cup milk
	Salt and pepper

In a small mixing bowl, whisk together the flour and milk until smooth. The batter should be just thick enough to adhere to the filling; thin with a little water, if necessary. Season to taste with salt and pepper.

FOR THE CROQUETTES	Salt
	6 medium Idaho potatoes
	20 medium shrimp, about 1 pound, peeled and deveined
	1 small Spanish onion, finely chopped (or substitute any white onion)
	¼ cup coarsely chopped fresh oregano
	2 tablespoons minced garlic
	4 teaspoons ground toasted fennel seed (page 45)
	4 tablespoons good-quality mayonnaise
	Pepper
	Peanut or canola oil, for frying
	Rice Flour Batter
	Yellow Pepper Relish (page 223)

Half fill a medium saucepan with water, add 1 tablespoon salt, and bring to a boil over high heat. Add the potatoes, reduce the heat to medium-high, and cook until tender, about 15 minutes. Drain, cool, and peel the potatoes.

Half fill a large saucepan with water, add 1 tablespoon salt, and bring to a boil over high heat. Add the shrimp, reduce the heat to medium-high, and blanch 3 minutes. Drain and coarsely chop.

Crumble the cooled potatoes into a large mixing bowl and add the onion, oregano, garlic, fennel, and mayonnaise. Mix well, being careful not to mash all the potatoes (you want some texture). Season to taste with salt and pepper and fold in the shrimp. Shape the mixture into 8 disks about 1 inch thick. Season to taste with salt and pepper.

In a large saucepan over high heat, heat ½ inch of oil to 375° F., or until a drop of batter sizzles on contact. Dip each croquette into batter, coating it lightly, and fry on both sides until crisp, about 4 minutes. Drain on paper towels.

Arrange on a platter and accompany with a bowl of relish.

Fried Squid with Anchovy Dressing and Parsley Pesto

MAKES 8 SERVINGS

The batter in this recipe is so light that you can see the fried squid right through it. I like serving two sauces alongside for dipping: strong and salty anchovy dressing cuts right through the richness of the squid, and green parsley pesto is a light and very herbaceous contrast.

The batter, anchovy dressing, and parsley pesto can all be prepared ahead. Fry the squid at the last minute before serving.

FOR THE ANCHOVY DRESSING

1	heaping tablespoon prepared mayonnaise
¾	cup sherry vinegar
1¾	cups pure olive oil
6	anchovy fillets
2	shallots, coarsely chopped
	Salt and pepper

In a blender or food processor, combine the mayonnaise, vinegar, oil, anchovies, and shallots and blend until smooth. Season to taste with salt and pepper. Makes about 3 cups. May be refrigerated up to 2 days; bring to room temperature before serving.

FOR THE PARSLEY PESTO

2	cups firmly packed parsley leaves
2	garlic cloves
2	tablespoons pumpkin seeds
2	tablespoons fresh lime juice
2	teaspoons salt
1	teaspoon pepper
5	tablespoons pure olive oil

In a food processor, combine the parsley, garlic, pumpkin seeds, lime juice, salt, and pepper. With the motor running, slowly add the olive oil until emulsified. Makes 1½ cups. May be refrigerated up to 2 days; bring to room temperature before serving.

FOR THE SQUID

8 **squid, cleaned and sliced into rings**
Salt and pepper
Rice Flour Batter (page 122)
4 **cups peanut oil**
Anchovy Dressing
Parsley Pesto

Season the squid with salt and pepper to taste and dip into the batter, allowing any excess to drip off.

In a large saucepan over high heat, heat the oil to 375° F., or until a drop of batter sizzles on contact. Fry the squid until crisp on all sides, about 4 minutes, and drain on paper towels. Pour the dressing onto a serving platter, stack the squid on top, and spoon dollops of pesto around them.

Oven-Roasted Tomato, Garlic, and Bread Soup

MAKES 8 SERVINGS

A hearty bread soup is a classic in Spain and Italy and a great way to recycle slightly stale bread. Make the base, a tomato and garlic soup, ahead of time. When your guests arrive, just kind of rip up the bread, put it in, heat it all up, and garnish, if you like, with crisp garlic chips. Bread is not a garnish here—it's an essential part of the soup.

FOR THE OVEN-ROASTED TOMATOES

4 plum tomatoes, halved lengthwise
2 garlic cloves, minced
2 tablespoons pure olive oil
Salt and pepper

Preheat the oven to 200°F.

Place the tomatoes cut-side up on a baking sheet. Combine the garlic and olive oil and brush the tomatoes with it, then season to taste with the salt and pepper. Roast until dried and soft, about 8 hours.

FOR THE SOUP

2	tablespoons pure olive oil
1	medium Spanish onion, chopped
½	cup white wine
4	quarts Chicken Stock (page 46) or canned low-sodium chicken broth
2	cups canned plum tomatoes
6	roasted garlic cloves (page 44)
	Oven-Roasted Tomatoes
2	tablespoons fresh thyme leaves
½	tablespoon honey
	Salt and white pepper
8	slices of French or Italian bread, about ½ inch thick, ripped into chunks
1	cup Toasted Garlic Chips (page 211), optional, for garnish

Heat the olive oil in a large saucepan over medium-high heat until it begins to smoke and sauté the onion until golden. Add the wine, raise the heat to high, and reduce until almost dry. Add the stock, canned tomatoes, roasted garlic, and roasted tomatoes and reduce by one-quarter.

Puree the mixture in a food processor and pour into a large pot. Add the thyme, honey, and salt and pepper to taste and set aside until just before serving time. Then add the bread, reheat over medium heat, and pour into a large serving bowl. Garnish with garlic chips, if desired.

Batter-Fried Potatoes

This classic Spanish dish can be prepared easily in the last minutes before serving—just take cooked new potatoes, throw them in some batter, and fry them. They are crisp and irresistible and they complement just about any dish you serve them with. Try some Saffron Mayonnaise in an earthenware bowl alongside.

FOR THE BEER BATTER

¾ cup beer
1 large egg, lightly beaten
¼ cup milk
1¼ cups all-purpose flour
1 tablespoon butter, melted
Salt and pepper

In a mixing bowl, combine the beer, egg, milk, flour, and melted butter and mix well. Add salt and pepper to taste. May be refrigerated up to 2 hours.

FOR THE POTATOES

10 medium new potatoes
2 tablespoons fresh thyme leaves
Beer Batter
½ cup seasoned flour (page 43)
Salt and pepper
4 cups peanut oil
1¼ cups Saffron Mayonnaise (page 218), optional

In a large pot of boiling salted water, cook the potatoes until just tender, about 20 minutes. Drain, peel, and slice ⅛ inch thick.

Add the thyme to the beer batter. Place the batter and the seasoned flour in 2 separate bowls. Season the potato slices with salt and pepper to taste.

In a sauté pan over medium heat, heat the oil to 375° F., or until a drop of batter sizzles on contact. Dredge the potato slices in the flour, dip them in the batter, and fry in batches until golden brown on both sides, about 2 minutes. Be sure not to crowd the potatoes in the pan. Drain on paper towels and season again with salt and pepper to taste. Place on a large serving platter. Accompany with saffron mayonnaise, if desired.

Green Onion Tamales

MAKES 10 TAMALES

Green onions accent the sweetness of fresh corn in this simple, clear combination of flavors and textures. Their flavor is echoed in the butter that melts into the fragrant, steaming filling (see color pages).

FOR THE GREEN ONION BUTTER	**6 tablespoons coarsely chopped green onions** **8 tablespoons (1 stick) butter** **Salt and pepper**

Blanch ¼ cup of the green onions until wilted in a large pot of boiling salted water over high heat, about 1 minute. Shock in a bowl of ice water and squeeze dry.

Combine the blanched onions, raw onions, butter, and salt and pepper to taste in a food processor and blend until smooth.

Place a sheet of parchment or wax paper on a work surface. Form the butter into a 1-inch-wide roll along the length of the paper, leaving a 1-inch border. Roll the butter up in the paper and refrigerate at least 30 minutes or up to 3 days, or freeze. Makes about 1 cup.

FOR THE TAMALES	**24 dried cornhusks (available at Hispanic markets)** **1½ cups fresh corn kernels (or substitute frozen)** **1 medium onion, coarsely chopped** **2 cups Chicken Stock (page 46), canned low-sodium chicken broth, or water** **6 tablespoons (¾ stick) butter** **6 tablespoons vegetable shortening** **1½ cups yellow cornmeal** **1½ teaspoons sugar** **Salt and pepper** **1 cup coarsely chopped green onions** **Green Onion Butter**

Rinse the cornhusks under running water. Soak them in warm water until softened, about 2 hours.

In a food processor, puree the corn, onion, and stock. Transfer the mixture to a mixing bowl and cut in the butter and shortening. Add the cornmeal, sugar, and salt and pepper to taste and combine well. (This masa mixture will be loose.)

Blanch the green onions until wilted in a large pot of boiling salted water over high heat, about 1 minute. Shock in a bowl of ice water and squeeze dry.

Add the blanched green onions to the masa mixture and combine well. Fill and tie the cornhusks as follows:

Drain the cornhusks; set aside the best 20 and pat dry. Tear the remaining husks into 1-inch-wide strips to be used for tying.

Lay 2 husks flat on a work surface, with the tapered ends facing out and the broad bases overlapping by about 3 inches. Place about $\frac{1}{3}$ cup masa in the center. Bring the long sides up over the masa, slightly overlapping, and pat down to close. (Don't worry if the masa leaks a bit at the seam.) Tie each end of the bundle with a strip of cornhusk, pushing the filling toward the middle. Trim the ends to about $\frac{1}{2}$ inch beyond the tie. The uncooked tamales can be refrigerated up to 1 hour.

Arrange the tamales in a single layer on a steaming rack, cover tightly with foil, and steam over boiling water 45 minutes. (Steamed tamales can be refrigerated up to 6 hours and reheated in a 350° F. oven 30 to 45 minutes.)

While the tamales are steaming, preheat the oven to 350° F. Bring the green onion butter to room temperature. Cut a slit on top of each tamale and push the ends toward the middle to expose the masa. Top each tamale with green onion butter and, if necessary, place in the oven until the butter has melted slightly, about 1 minute. Arrange on a large serving platter.

Plantain Tamales with Molasses Butter

MAKES 10 TAMALES

Cuban and Mexican influences come together here in a beautiful centerpiece for a party table. Cook ripe plantains with brown sugar and molasses, puree them, and fold them into masa, a cornmeal batter. Then wrap the mixture in dried cornhusks and cook over steaming water. Let a little sweet molasses butter melt into the steamed masa, then serve these with anything—literally.

FOR THE MOLASSES BUTTER

- **¼ cup dark molasses**
- **1 tablespoon maple syrup**
- **8 tablespoons (1 stick) butter, at room temperature**
- **Salt and pepper**

In a food processor, blend the molasses, maple syrup, butter, and salt and pepper to taste until smooth. The mixture will be soft.

Place a sheet of parchment or wax paper about 12 by 12 inches on a work surface. Form the butter into a 1-inch-wide roll along the length of the paper, leaving a 1-inch border at the top and bottom. Roll the butter up in the paper and refrigerate at least 30 minutes or up to 3 days, or freeze. Makes about 1 cup.

24	dried cornhusks
8	tablespoons butter
4	ripe plantains, peeled and cut into small dice
3	tablespoons light brown sugar
2	tablespoons molasses
1½	cups fresh corn kernels (or substitute frozen)
1	medium onion, coarsely chopped
2	cups Chicken Stock (page 46), canned low-sodium chicken broth, or water
6	tablespoons vegetable shortening
1½	cups yellow cornmeal
1½	teaspoons sugar
	Salt and pepper
1	cup Molasses Butter

Rinse the cornhusks under running water. Soak them in warm water until softened, about 2 hours.

Melt 2 tablespoons of butter in a large sauté pan over medium heat and add the diced plantains. Add the brown sugar and molasses and cook until they form a syrupy glaze.

In a food processor, puree the corn, onion, and stock. Transfer the mixture to a mixing bowl and cut in the remaining 6 tablespoons of butter and the shortening. Add the cornmeal, sugar, and salt and pepper to taste. (The masa mixture will be loose.) Add the plantains and combine well.

Fill and tie the cornhusks as follows:

Drain the cornhusks; set aside the best 20 and pat dry. Tear the remaining husks into 1-inch-wide strips to be used for tying.

Lay 2 husks flat on a work surface, with the tapered ends facing out and the broad bases overlapping by about 3 inches. Place about ⅓ cup masa in the center. Bring the long sides up over the masa, slightly overlapping, and pat down to close. (Don't worry if the masa leaks a bit at the seam.) Tie each end of the bundle with a strip of cornhusk, pushing the filling toward the middle. Trim the ends to about ½ inch beyond the tie. The uncooked tamales can be refrigerated up to 1 hour.

Arrange the tamales in a single layer on a steaming rack, cover tightly with foil, and steam over boiling water 45 minutes. (Steamed tamales can be refrigerated up to 6 hours and reheated in a 350° F. oven 30 to 45 minutes.)

While the tamales are steaming, preheat the oven to 350° F. and bring the molasses butter to room temperature. Cut a slit on top of each tamale and push the ends toward the middle to expose the masa. Top each tamale with a pat of molasses butter and, if necessary, place in the oven until the butter has melted slightly, about 1 minute. Arrange on a large serving platter.

Spicy and Sweet Rum Plantains

MAKES 8 SERVINGS

Cuban influence is evident in this combination of plantains with rum and honey. Spicy ancho chile powder for searing the plantains adds a jolt of energy.

- 4 tablespoons (½ stick) butter
- 4 very ripe medium plantains (they should be almost black), peeled and sliced ¼ inch thick on the bias
- 2 teaspoons ancho chile powder (available at Hispanic or specialty markets)
- Salt and pepper
- ½ cup dark rum
- 1 heaping tablespoon honey

Melt 2 tablespoons of the butter in a large sauté pan over medium-high heat. Dust the plantains with the ancho chile powder and sear about 1 minute on each side. Season to taste with salt and pepper.

Drain the plantains on paper towels and place on a serving platter. Pour the rum into the pan and reduce 1 minute over high heat. Add the honey and the remaining 2 tablespoons of butter, stir well, and season to taste with salt and pepper. Pour the mixture over the plantains and serve immediately.

Broccoli Rabe with Caramelized Shallots

MAKES 8 SERVINGS

When I first tasted broccoli rabe, I was a little put off by its bitterness, so I combined it with some golden caramelized shallots. They add just the right note of sweetness and provide contrasting texture as well (see color pages).

FOR THE CARAMELIZED SHALLOTS

2 tablespoons (¼ stick) butter
6 shallots, peeled and sliced into ⅛-inch rounds
¼ cup balsamic vinegar
1 tablespoon honey
Salt and pepper

Melt the butter in a medium saucepan over medium heat. Add the shallots, vinegar, and honey and cook, stirring, until the vinegar has reduced and coated the shallots, about 10 minutes. Season to taste with salt and pepper.

FOR THE BROCCOLI RABE

2 tablespoons pure olive oil
1½ pounds broccoli rabe (about 2 bunches), washed well and bottom of stems trimmed
½ cup water
Caramelized Shallots
Salt and pepper

Heat the oil in a large sauté pan over high heat until it begins to smoke and add the broccoli rabe, water, and caramelized shallots. Cook, stirring, until the broccoli rabe is wilted and the shallots are hot, 5 to 7 minutes. Season with salt and pepper to taste and place in a large serving bowl.

love all kinds of rice dishes, from the stark to the complex. Besides being delicious on its own, rice goes with just about everything and can be the underpinning for any number of other foods. When you serve my Latin dishes, it's a good idea to have some kind of rice on the table to round out the mix.

Cilantro Rice, Wild Mushroom Rice, and Saffron-Tomato Rice are the simplest combinations I present. In them, the grains are fluffy and separate, the herbal and vegetable flavors remain distinct, and all the textures are fairly well defined. These make good base dishes for fish, shellfish, or fowl— try grilled fish or shrimp on top of Cilantro Rice, roasted chicken over Wild Mushroom Rice, and lobster over Saffron-Tomato Rice.

Paella, one of the most famous rice dishes in the world, moves in another direction, letting its flavors and textures merge and influence one another. The base of paella is usually some kind of sausage with some kind of rice, but you can experiment with more imaginative combinations of ingredients: flavor the rice with saffron (the classic version) or curry; start with Wild Mushroom Rice instead of plain rice; include game birds or fish. Be flexible with vegetables and add the best of the season: in spring and summer, try asparagus; in the winter, peas. When you put a brilliant paella on the table, it's a one-dish meal.

Paella's Italian cousin, risotto, blends perfectly with Latin flavors like black beans or roasted rabbit and it makes a variety of beautiful party dishes. In risotto, the rice is cooked until it is creamy and the grains run into each other. Within its creaminess, all the ingredients meld together.

Unfortunately, lots of otherwise daring cooks seem to be intimidated by risotto. Whenever I demonstrate it for a cooking class, I hear cries of: "Oh, no! It's so hard to make!" What are these people talking about? You stand over it and stir; if it gets dry, you add liquid. The only trick is to keep stirring.

This is what I tell my classes: Start with a wide pot, like a rondeau, that will give you a good stirring surface, and sweat finely minced onions and garlic in it. In another pot, have some stock simmering. You can use chicken, fish, or shellfish stock as a cooking liquid, or, if the other ingredients are strongly flavored, it's fine to use plain water.

Then all you need are rice and a wooden spoon. Cover the rice with simmering liquid and stir over medium-high heat until it starts to thicken and dry up a little bit. When this happens, add more liquid—you will hear a hiss, like the sound of a cappuccino machine—and keep stirring. Repeat until the risotto gets to the right consistency: al dente, creamy, with a little sauce bubbling at the bottom of the pan.

Stir in the other ingredients, such as charred yellow tomato puree, sweet potato puree, or Black Olive Tapenade, when the rice is cooked and then bring the dish to the table immediately. Risotto should be the last thing you prepare, because once it is done, it can't wait.

The process should take about 20 minutes, although it can take longer. I cook risotto in 12 minutes on high heat, but I wouldn't advise trying it that way until you have the technique down perfectly, or you will get burned rice. Cooking on medium-high heat takes longer, but it's safer.

To make things even easier, you can partially prepare risotto up to a day ahead. Cook the rice using three-quarters of the liquid, making sure you undercook, and then spread it on a sheet pan. Take care to spread it evenly, which will allow it all to cool at the same time. Then cover it and refrigerate. When you're ready for dinner, put the partially cooked rice into a saucepan with the remaining hot stock over medium-high heat. Break it up and stir until the stock is absorbed and the rice is hot. Add the rest of the ingredients and serve immediately.

Cilantro Rice

Cilantro is a strong herb with a fresh, pungent flavor. Often people don't like it at first taste but I always encourage them to try it again, and most of them change their minds. In addition to its herbal taste, this green rice also is flavored with clam juice and garlic, making it a savory bed for grilled fish or a delicious partner for smoky grilled shrimp (see color pages).

FOR THE HERBAL BROTH	
2	cups clam juice
1	cup spinach, blanched (page 44)
1	cup cilantro, blanched (page 44)
	Salt and pepper
1/2	teaspoon honey, or to taste

Place the clam juice, spinach, and cilantro in a blender and puree. Strain through a fine strainer and season to taste with salt, pepper, and honey. Makes 2½ cups. May be refrigerated up to 2 days.

FOR THE RICE	
2	tablespoons (¼ stick) butter
3	cloves garlic, finely chopped
3	cups converted white rice
3½	cups water
	Herbal Broth
	Salt and pepper
1/2	cup coarsely chopped cilantro

Melt the butter in a medium saucepan over low heat and cook the garlic until translucent. Add the rice and stir to coat. Add the water and herbal broth and season to taste with salt and pepper. Cover the pan and cook 12 to 15 minutes, or until cooked through. Stir in the cilantro.

Lemon-Thyme Rice

MAKES 8 SERVINGS

Lemon and thyme add citric and herbal flavors to this textured mixture of wild and white rice. Serve this rice along with any fish dish (see color pages).

1½ cups wild rice cooked in 4½ cups lightly salted Chicken Stock (page 46) or canned low-sodium chicken broth

1½ cups converted white rice cooked in 3 cups lightly salted Chicken Stock or canned low-sodium chicken broth

Juice and zest of 1 lemon

1 cup Chicken Stock or canned low-sodium chicken broth

2 tablespoons fresh thyme leaves

1 tablespoon honey

Salt and pepper

1 cup peeled, seeded, diced tomato

In a large sauté pan over medium-high heat, combine the wild rice, white rice, lemon juice and zest, stock, and thyme. Cook until the mixture is heated through and the liquid has evaporated. Add the honey and season to taste with the salt and pepper. Fold in the tomato.

Wild Mushroom Rice

MAKES 8 SERVINGS

*Wild Mushroom Rice is simply one of the best things you can eat.
All these wild mushrooms and their juices just sort of fall into the rice
and drench it with flavor. It's earthy and fantastic on its own or as a
bed for roasted chicken.*

> **5** tablespoons butter
> **½** pound shiitake mushrooms, stems removed
>   and caps cut **¼** inch thick
> **2** large portobello mushrooms, stems removed and
>   caps cut **¼** inch thick
> **½** pound oyster mushrooms, stems removed
>   and caps cut **¼** inch thick
>   Salt and pepper
> **1** tablespoon pure olive oil
> **1** medium Spanish onion, finely diced
> **3** cups converted white rice
> **6** cups Chicken Stock (page 46) or canned low-sodium
>   chicken broth
> **⅓** cup porcini mushroom powder (ground dried porcini
>   mushrooms, available at specialty food stores)

Melt 3 tablespoons of the butter in a large sauté pan over medium-high heat and sauté the mushrooms until tender. Season to taste with salt and pepper and set aside to cool.

In a medium saucepan, heat the remaining butter with the olive oil until almost smoking and sauté the onion until tender. Add the rice and stir to coat with the butter and oil. Add the stock, 1 teaspoon salt, and the porcini powder. Cover and cook until the rice is cooked through, 15 to 18 minutes. Fold in the reserved mushroom mixture, season to taste with salt and pepper, and keep warm, covered with foil. Or refrigerate up to 2 days and rewarm over low heat.

Saffron-Tomato Rice

MAKES 8 SERVINGS

Saffron gives rice a perfumed, flowery note and a classic Spanish flavor, and it has a great affinity for tomatoes. Try Saffron-Tomato Rice as a bed for grilled, boiled, or steamed lobster (see color pages).

6 cups water
Salt
Large pinch of saffron threads
1 tablespoon butter
1 tablespoon pure olive oil
1 medium Spanish onion, diced
3 cups converted white rice
10 medium tomatoes, seeded and diced
Pepper

Combine the water, 2 tablespoons salt, and saffron in a medium pot over high heat and simmer until the threads open and color and flavor the water, 5 to 8 minutes.

Melt the butter and oil in a medium saucepan over medium-high heat and sauté the onion until tender. Add the rice and stir to coat with the oil and butter. Add the saffron broth, cover, and reduce the heat to medium. Cook until the rice is tender, about 15 minutes. Fold in the tomatoes and season to taste with salt and pepper.

Black Beans and Rice

Black beans with rice has a long history as a Spanish staple. Although sometimes the combination can be kind of bland, this version is herbaceous and colorful, with lots of bright green basil. It's great in the center of a table, surrounded by compatible dishes (almost anything suits it). Although at first glance it seems to resemble Black Bean Risotto (page 152), here the beans remain separate and chunky.

1 **pound dried black beans, picked over**
1 **ham hock or ½ cup ham scraps**
1 **12-ounce bottle ale or beer**
¼ **cup plus 3 tablespoons pure olive oil**
1 **medium onion, finely diced**
1½ **cups converted white rice**
3 **cups water**
Salt
2 **cups fresh basil leaves**
2 **tablespoons pine nuts**
8 **roasted garlic cloves (page 44)**
1 **cup olive oil**
½ **cup grated Grana Padano cheese (or substitute Parmesan)**
Pepper
Chopped parsley, for garnish

Soak the beans overnight in double their volume of water. Drain and place in a large, heavy pot with double their volume of water, the ham, and beer. Cook over medium-high heat until tender, about 1 hour. Drain and spread on a large baking sheet to cool.

Heat 3 tablespoons of the olive oil in a large saucepan over medium heat until it begins to smoke and sweat the onion about 3 minutes. Add the rice and cook, stirring, until it is coated with the oil, about 3 minutes. Add the water and 1 tablespoon salt, stir, and bring to a boil. Lower the heat and simmer until the water is absorbed and the rice is tender.

Place the basil in a food processor with the pine nuts and roasted garlic. With the motor running, slowly add the olive oil, making a smooth paste.

Combine the cooked rice and beans in a large sauce pot or sauté pan, add water to cover, and cook over medium heat until almost dry. Add the pesto and stir to incorporate. Stir in the cheese and season to taste with salt and pepper. Place in a large serving bowl and garnish with chopped parsley. Serve hot.

Curried Shellfish and Chicken Paella

MAKES 8 SERVINGS

You make this dish and that's the party. Sangria, paella—done!
I flavor the rice with curry instead of saffron because I like the way the
combination of fiery spices enhances the clams, lobster, and mussels.
If you want to make the classic version, see the variation on page 150.

The key to paella is doing different parts of it at different times.
If you cook everything together, as is usually done, something always
gets overcooked and something always ends up undercooked. A better
way is to cook each component separately, then put them together and
let the flavors marry for a little while at the end, just as your guests
arrive (see color pages).

FOR THE RICE

- ½ **pound chorizo, sliced**
- 3 **tablespoons pure olive oil**
- 1 **medium onion, diced**
- 2 **tablespoons good-quality curry powder**
- 1 **tablespoon turmeric**
- 1 **tablespoon ancho chile powder (available at Hispanic or specialty markets)**
- 4 **cups converted white rice**
- 8 **cups water**
- 2 **tablespoons honey**
- **Salt and pepper**

Cook the chorizo in a large saucepan over medium-high heat until browned and the fat is rendered out. Remove the chorizo to a plate lined with paper towels and pour off the fat.

Return the saucepan to the stove and heat the olive oil over medium-high heat until almost smoking. Add the onion, curry powder, turmeric, and ancho chile powder and sauté 3 to 4 minutes. Add the rice and stir until coated. Add the chorizo and water, cover, and cook until the rice is al dente. Add the honey and season to taste with salt and pepper.

If not completing the dish immediately, cook the rice with only three-quarters of the liquid and spread on a sheet pan to cool. May be refrigerated up to 1 day. To reheat, put the partially cooked rice in a saucepan with the remaining hot cooking liquid over medium-high heat. Break it up and stir until the stock is absorbed and the rice is hot.

FOR THE PAELLA	
24	cultivated mussels, debearded
16	littleneck clams
32	asparagus spears
	Salt and pepper
8	chicken thighs
2	lobsters, about 1¼ pounds each
2	tablespoons pure olive oil, plus extra for brushing
8	large sea scallops
8	shrimp, heads on

Steam the mussels, clams, and asparagus in ½ inch of water in a large stockpot over medium-high heat until the asparagus is crisp and the shellfish open, discarding any that do not open. Season to taste with salt and pepper. May be refrigerated up to 2 hours.

While the shellfish are steaming, preheat the oven to 500° F. Season the chicken with salt and pepper to taste and place in a baking pan. Roast until cooked through, 20 to 25 minutes.

Kill the lobsters by inserting a sharp knife into the cross mark on the top shell between the head and the body. Pull or cut off the claws. Pull or cut off the tails and cut in half lengthwise. (Discard the bodies.) Season with salt and pepper to taste, brush with pure olive oil, and place in a baking pan. Roast until cooked through, 10 to 15 minutes. May be refrigerated up to 1 day.

While the chicken and lobster are roasting, season the scallops and shrimp with salt and pepper to taste. Heat 2 tablespoons olive oil in a medium-size sauté pan or skillet over medium-high heat until almost smoking. Sear the scallops 8 to 10 seconds on each side; sear the shrimp 15 seconds on each side.

To serve, spoon the rice mixture onto a large platter and top with the chicken, shellfish, and asparagus. If the ingredients have been cooked ahead, reheat the rice as described above, reheat the other components in separate pans in a 400°F. oven, and combine.

Classic Paella

VARIATION

For a saffron-flavored paella, omit the curry powder, turmeric, chile powder, and honey and substitute 1 tablespoon saffron threads.

Black Bean Risotto

MAKES 8 SERVINGS

Here is a play on the Cuban classic black beans and rice, but transformed by a touch of spicy chipotles, honey, and herbs. Arborio rice, the kind used for risotto, is simmered with cooked black beans that infuse it with flavor. The finished dish is creamy, with the black beans melting into the rice.

> 5 cups Chicken Stock (page 46) or canned low-sodium chicken broth (or use part water)
> 1 cup white wine
> 4 tablespoons (½ stick) butter
> 1 large Spanish onion, diced
> 1 head of roasted garlic, mashed (page 44), or 1 head of raw garlic, minced
> 2 cups arborio rice
> ½ pound black beans, cooked and drained (page 146), or substitute 2¾ cups drained canned beans
> 2 tablespoons honey
> 1 tablespoon chipotle puree (page 42)
> ¼ cup chopped green onions
> ¼ cup chopped cilantro leaves
> Salt and pepper
> ¼ cup grated Parmesan cheese

Combine the stock and wine in a saucepan over medium-high heat and bring to a boil. Reduce the heat to medium and keep the broth simmering.

Melt the butter in a large pot over medium-high heat and sweat the onion and garlic. Add the rice and toss to coat with the butter. Cook the rice until lightly toasted.

Add 1 cup of stock and cook, stirring, until it is absorbed. Repeat with a second cup. As the rice becomes dry, add stock in $\frac{1}{2}$-cup increments, cooking and stirring until it is absorbed.

When the rice is about three-quarters cooked, mix in the beans, honey, chipotle puree, green onions, and cilantro. Continue cooking, adding broth as needed, until al dente and creamy, with a little liquid on the bottom of the pot.

Season to taste with salt and pepper and stir in the Parmesan cheese. Pour onto a large platter and serve immediately.

Charred Yellow Tomato Risotto

MAKES 8 SERVINGS

Summer's golden tomatoes have a light, fruity taste and very little acidity. Charring on a grill or in a broiler gives them the flavor boost they need. This risotto goes well with grilled fish, shrimp, or chicken and a good white wine (see color pages).

FOR THE CHARRED YELLOW TOMATO PUREE	2 **large yellow tomatoes** 1 **tablespoon pure olive oil** **Salt and pepper**

In a small mixing bowl, toss the tomatoes with the oil and season to taste with the salt and pepper.

Sear the tomatoes in a stovetop grill pan over high heat, or under the broiler, turning until black on all sides. Peel off the charred skin and remove the seeds.

Puree the tomato pulp in a food processor. May be refrigerated up to 3 days.

FOR THE RISOTTTO	7½ **cups Chicken Stock (page 46) or canned low-sodium chicken broth (or use part water)** 6 **tablespoons (¾ stick) butter** ¼ **cup pure olive oil** 1 **medium Spanish onion, finely diced** 1 **tablespoon minced garlic** 3 **cups arborio rice** **Charred Yellow Tomato Puree** 1¼ **cups grated Grana Padano cheese (or substitute good-quality Parmesan)** **Salt and pepper** 1 **medium yellow tomato, finely diced**

Bring the stock to a simmer in a medium saucepan.

Melt 4 tablespoons of the butter with the olive oil in a large saucepan over medium-high heat. Add the onion and garlic and sweat until translucent, about 4 minutes. Add the rice and stir until coated with the butter and oil.

Add 1 cup of the stock and cook, stirring, until absorbed. Repeat with a second cup. As the rice becomes dry, add stock in $\frac{1}{2}$-cup increments, cooking and stirring until it is absorbed. Add the puree, the remaining 2 tablespoons of butter, and 1 cup of the cheese. Mix well and season to taste with salt and pepper.

Place on a serving platter and top with the diced tomato and the remaining cheese. Serve immediately.

Saffron Risotto with Grilled Shrimp and Green Onion Vinaigrette

MAKES 8 SERVINGS

It takes a little finesse to get all the parts of this dish on the table at roughly the same time. First, you can make the Green Onion Vinaigrette up to 2 days ahead. Start the risotto shortly before serving time, and as you're finishing it, just toss the shrimp on the grill (which you have already started up). It will all come together, I promise. To serve, mound the risotto in a bowl, throw the shrimp on top, and splash everything with the vinaigrette.

FOR THE RISOTTO	
8	cups Lobster or Shrimp Stock (page 47), or use part water
¼	cup pure olive oil
½	medium Spanish onion, finely chopped
1	tablespoon minced garlic
2	cups white wine
2	cups arborio rice
1	tablespoon saffron threads
1	tablespoon honey
2	tablespoons coarsely chopped fresh tarragon
	Salt and pepper

Bring the stock to a simmer in a saucepan.

Heat the olive oil in a large saucepan over medium heat and sweat the onion and garlic until softened but not colored, about 4 minutes. Raise the heat to high, add the wine, and reduce until dry. Reduce the heat, add the rice and saffron, and stir until the rice is coated with the oil. Cook 2 minutes.

Add 1 cup of the stock and cook, stirring, until absorbed. Repeat with a second cup. As the rice becomes dry, add stock in $\frac{1}{2}$-cup increments, cooking and stirring until it is absorbed. Add the honey and tarragon and season to taste with salt and pepper.

FOR THE GRILLED SHRIMP	**24 large shrimp** **Pure olive oil, for rubbing shrimp** **Salt and pepper**

Prepare a grill or preheat the broiler.

Rub the shrimp with olive oil and season to taste with salt and pepper. Grill approximately 3 minutes on each side.

TO ASSEMBLE	**Green Onion Vinaigrette (page 205)**

Spoon the risotto into a large serving bowl. Arrange the shrimp over it and drizzle the green onion vinaigrette over all. Serve the remaining vinaigrette on the side.

Fresh Green Pea and Toasted Coriander Risotto

MAKES 8 SERVINGS

This is a good spring and summer risotto. You can serve it as is or add some grilled shrimp and make it the center of your table (see color pages).

FOR THE LEEK BROTH

2 tablespoons (¼ stick) butter
2 medium leeks, cleaned and sliced thin (white and green parts)
1 medium Spanish onion, sliced thin
6 shallots, sliced thin
2 tablespoons minced garlic
1 cup white wine
4 cups Fish Stock (page 46) or clam juice (or use part water)

Melt the butter in a large saucepan over medium-high heat and sweat the leeks, onion, shallots, and garlic 1 minute. Add the wine, raise the heat to high, and reduce by three-quarters. Add the stock and mix well. Refrigerate until cool; strain. Makes 4 cups. May be refrigerated up to 2 days.

FOR THE PEA PUREE

2 cups thawed frozen peas
⅔ cup Leek Broth

Puree the peas and broth in a food processor.

4 tablespoons (½ stick) butter
1 large Spanish onion, finely chopped
1 head of roasted garlic (page 44),
   separated into cloves
1 cup dry white wine
3 cups arborio rice
   Leek Broth, plus enough water to make 7 cups
1 tablespoon toasted coriander seeds, ground
   (page 45)
1 tablespoon chopped chives
1 teaspoon grated lemon zest
1 cup fresh peas
¼ cup grated Grana Padano cheese (or substitute
   good-quality Parmesan)
   Salt and pepper
   Pea Puree

Melt the butter in a large saucepan over medium-high heat and sweat the onion and garlic until softened but not colored, about 4 minutes. Raise the heat to high, add the wine, and reduce until dry. Reduce the heat, add the rice, and stir to coat the rice with the butter.

Add 1 cup of the broth and cook, stirring, until absorbed. Repeat with a second cup. As the rice becomes dry, add stock in ½-cup increments, cooking and stirring until it is absorbed. Add the coriander, chives, and lemon zest. Add the peas, cheese, and salt and pepper to taste. Stir in the pea puree and place in a large serving bowl.

Black Olive Risotto

Black Olive Risotto was the first dish I thought of when we opened Bolo, because it represents the kind of food that the restaurant stands for: updated and modern, but with traditional flavors preserved. Serve this risotto with chicken, beef, pork, tuna, or swordfish.

6 cups Chicken Stock (page 46) or canned low-sodium chicken broth (or use part water)
¼ cup pure olive oil
1 medium Spanish onion, finely chopped (or substitute white onion)
1 tablespoon minced garlic
2 cups white wine
3 cups arborio rice
1 cup Black Olive Tapenade (page 220)
¼ cup coarsely chopped parsley
1 tablespoon honey
Salt and pepper

Bring the stock to a simmer in a medium saucepan.

Heat the olive oil in a large sauté pan over medium-high heat until it begins to smoke. Add the onion and garlic and sweat until translucent, about 4 minutes. Add the wine and cook, stirring well, until most of it is absorbed. Add the rice and stir until coated with the oil. Be sure to scrape the bottom of the pan so the rice doesn't burn.

Add 1 cup of stock and cook, stirring, until absorbed. Repeat with a second cup. As the rice becomes dry, add stock in ½-cup increments, cooking and stirring until it is absorbed. Add the tapenade, parsley, and honey and season to taste with salt and pepper. The risotto will be a little loose, but will thicken once it is removed from the heat.

Place on a serving platter and serve immediately.

Sweet Potato and Pine Nut Risotto with Roasted Rabbit and Black Olive Vinaigrette

MAKES 8 SERVINGS

A meal in itself, this is kind of a cross between paella and risotto. It's a delicious mélange of sweet potatoes, pine nuts, and savory rabbit, all flavored with a pungent Black Olive Vinaigrette. This is a big dish!

FOR THE RABBIT	**8 rabbit legs**
	4 rabbit loins
	Salt and pepper
	½ cup pure olive oil
	1 large Spanish onion, coarsely chopped
	1 large carrot, coarsely chopped
	2 celery stalks, coarsely chopped
	2 cups red wine
	2 cups port wine

Preheat the oven to 400°F.

Season the rabbit with salt and pepper to taste. Heat ¼ cup olive oil in a large skillet over high heat until smoking and sear the meat until lightly browned, about 3 minutes on each side. Remove from the pan.

Add the onion, carrot, and celery to the pan, reduce the heat to medium, and cook 5 minutes. Add the red wine and port wine and return the rabbit to the pan. Cover and braise until fork-tender, about 1 hour. Remove the meat and cut each loin into 3 pieces. Strain and reserve the cooking liquid.

Place the loins and legs in a baking dish with 2 cups of the reserved cooking liquid and roast 9 minutes. Reserve all cooking liquid for the risotto.

FOR THE SWEET POTATO PUREE	1 medium sweet potato, peeled and quartered 2 tablespoons honey

Place the sweet potato with water to cover in a small saucepan over high heat and bring to a boil. Reduce the heat to medium and simmer until tender, about 15 minutes. Drain, and puree in a food processor or blender with the honey.

FOR THE SWEET POTATO AND PINE NUT RISOTTO	Braising liquid from cooking the rabbit 6 tablespoons (¾ stick) butter ¼ cup pure olive oil 2 rabbit livers 1 medium Spanish onion, finely chopped 3 cups arborio rice 4 tablespoons Sweet Potato Puree 1 cup plus 4 tablespoons grated Grana Padano cheese (or substitute good-quality Parmesan) Salt and pepper 1 large tomato, seeded and diced 4 tablespoons pine nuts, toasted 4 tablespoons coarsely chopped chives ¼ cup Black Olive Vinaigrette (page 200)

Measure the braising liquid and add enough water to make 7½ cups. Bring to a simmer in a medium saucepan.

Heat 4 tablespoons of the butter with the olive oil in a large saucepan over medium to high heat until almost smoking and sear the livers 1 minute on each side. Cool the livers, dice, and reserve.

Add the onion to the pan and sweat until translucent, about 4 minutes. Add the rice and cook, stirring, 3 minutes. Add 1 cup of the braising liquid and cook, stirring, until absorbed. Repeat the process until all the liquid has been added and absorbed.

Add the sweet potato puree, 1 cup of the cheese, the diced rabbit livers, and the remaining 2 tablespoons butter and combine. Season to taste with salt and pepper.

Place in a large serving bowl or platter and garnish with the tomato, pine nuts, chives, and the remaining cheese. Spoon the black olive vinaigrette over the top.

Wild Rice and Goat Cheese Stuffing

MAKES 8 SERVINGS

Celery, onion, carrots, and garlic are the classic stuffing vegetables and, for a Latin note, I add crisp and spicy chorizo to them. I put some goat cheese in the mix because I love it and it goes really well with wild rice, but if you don't like goat cheese, just leave it out.

It is important that the mixture be quite wet when you put it in the oven—probably wetter than you think it should be. Spoon it into a baking dish and bake for 25 to 30 minutes at the very most. Everything in it is already cooked and you are just heating it through. You want it to become a little brown on top and to have a nice texture, but you don't want it to dry out in the oven. You can do this stuffing a day ahead. To reheat in the oven, spoon a little chicken stock on top, cover with foil, and steam it back to life.

- 1½ cups wild rice (do not use long-grain and wild rice)
- 5 cups water
- Salt
- ½ cup coarsely diced chorizo
- 4 tablespoons (½ stick) butter, plus extra for greasing the baking dish
- 1 large onion, finely diced
- 2 tablespoons minced garlic
- 2 carrots, chopped fine
- 3 celery stalks, chopped fine
- 1 small loaf (1 pound) day-old or stale country-style white bread, cubed
- 6 ounces goat cheese
- 3 tablespoons fresh thyme leaves (or substitute parsley, sage, or oregano)
- 1½ cups Chicken Stock (page 46), canned low-sodium chicken broth, or water, plus extra, if needed
- Pepper

Place the rice, water, and salt to taste in a medium saucepan and bring to a boil over medium-high heat. Simmer until the grains open all the way. Drain the rice.

Meanwhile, cook the chorizo in a small saucepan over medium heat until the fat is rendered and the chorizo gets a little crisp. Drain.

Preheat the oven to 350° F.

Melt the butter in a large sauté pan over medium heat. Add the onion, garlic, carrots, and celery and sweat until the onion is tender, about 5 minutes. Add the rice, chorizo, bread, cheese, thyme, and stock and stir to combine. The mixture should be quite wet; add a little more stock or water, if needed. Season to taste with salt and pepper.

Transfer to a 6-cup buttered baking dish and bake, uncovered, until golden brown and heated through, 25 to 30 minutes. May be refrigerated up to 1 day; reheat with a little chicken stock for 20 minutes at 350° F. Serve alongside roasted turkey with pomegranate sauce (page 211).

olters

If your party needs a few beautiful dishes that can be done ahead and forgotten until your guests arrive, it needs cool platters! These are the greatest for entertaining, because they require little, if any, last-minute effort. Cool platters may be salady things, like mizuna greens combined with cheese, sausage, or wild mushrooms. They may highlight cooked vegetables, like roasted eggplant, or a salad of baked cabbage with haricots verts, or they may combine grains, rice, or potatoes with spicy or herbal dressings. A cool platter can be a complex jumble of fruit, seafood, cheese, and fresh herbs or a perfectly simple Carpaccio of Beef.

Many of these dishes are cool straight through, like Octopus and Chickpea Salad or Spicy Jumbo Lump Crab and Black Bean Salad with Roasted Red Pepper Sauce and Cilantro Oil, but they also can be clever combinations of warm and cold. When cool greens play off against warm baked eggplant or cool fruit accents sautéed or grilled squid, your palate is pleasantly surprised. And since warm ingredients aren't the same as hot, they don't have to be done at the last minute.

Not only is there a subtle range of temperatures in these platters, the variety of textures adds another kind of interest. In Sophie's Salad, crunchy tortillas set off smooth cheese, crisp lettuce, chewy beans and chickpeas, and

juicy tomatoes. Red and yellow gazpacho contrasts smooth pureed tomatoes and peppers with dense, juicy grilled scallops.

A cool platter presents many flavors, each separate and outspoken. So you can have chorizo, Cabrales blue cheese, greens, and tomatoes heaped on one plate and saffron-flavored rice, asparagus, roasted peppers, all in a Sweet and Fiery Dressing, on another. Grilled Squid and Vidalia Onion Salad with Roasted Tomatoes and Green Chile Vinaigrette describes itself pretty well— and it also has some fresh mint.

These aren't wimpy salads, shyly sitting next to your more boisterous creations— each is substantial and has a voice of its own. If you decide to ignore hot dishes and spread the table with cool platters only, as I often do, there will be plenty of variety in flavor, color, texture, and even in temperature. These platters won't require a lot of skill or patience to assemble because their presentation is meant to be relaxed. A bouquet of colorful ingredients tossed together with spirit will set the mood for an informal table and party.

Bolo Salad with Chorizo, Cabrales Blue Cheese, and Tomatoes

MAKES 8 SERVINGS

Sweet, juicy tomatoes, spicy chorizo, and the sharp and creamy complexity of Cabrales blue cheese—the best blue cheese in the world— highlight Bolo's house salad (see color pages).

FOR THE CROUTONS

16 slices of French or Italian bread, cut ½ inch thick
¼ cup pure olive oil
    Salt and pepper

Preheat the oven to 350°F. Brush the bread with the oil and arrange on a baking sheet. Sprinkle with salt and pepper and bake until lightly browned on both sides, about 7 minutes. Makes 16 croutons.

FOR THE SALAD

1 pound chorizo sausage, sliced ⅛ inch thick
8 cups mixed greens, rinsed well and dried
1 cup Sherry Vinaigrette (page 207)
    Salt and pepper
2 medium tomatoes, each cut into 8 slices
16 croutons
8 ounces Cabrales blue cheese

In a small skillet over low heat, cook the sausage until the fat is rendered, about 10 minutes. Drain on paper towels.

Place the greens in a large bowl, add the dressing, and mix well. Season to taste with salt and pepper and garnish with the chorizo and tomatoes. Surround with croutons spread with the cheese.

Sophie's Salad

MAKES 8 SERVINGS

*This vivid salad is named for my beautiful daughter. It has so many ingredients, all these different things going on—*exactly *like Sophie.*

FOR THE TORTILLA CHIPS

2 **cups peanut oil**
2 **6-inch blue corn tortillas, cut into ½-inch squares**
2 **6-inch yellow corn tortillas, cut into ½-inch squares**

In a saucepan, heat the peanut oil to 360°F., or until a bit of tortilla sizzles on contact. Fry the tortilla squares until crisp, about 30 seconds, and drain on paper towels.

FOR THE SALAD

6 **cups finely chopped romaine lettuce**
2 **tomatoes, finely diced**
½ **cup cooked or canned red beans**
½ **cup cooked or canned chickpeas**
½ **cup pitted niçoise olives**
½ **pound white Cheddar cheese, cut into ½-inch cubes**
½ **pound Monterey Jack cheese, cut into ½-inch cubes**
Balsamic-Mustard Vinaigrette (page 209)
Tortilla chips

In a large bowl, combine the lettuce, tomatoes, beans, chickpeas, olives, and cheeses. Dress lightly with the vinaigrette and sprinkle with the tortilla chips.

Wild Mushroom and Mizuna Salad with White Truffle Vinaigrette and Sage

MAKES 8 SERVINGS

To dress these delicate greens, squirt or spoon the vinaigrette around the inside of the bowl and move the greens up into the dressing, coating them lightly. Don't overdress the salad—keep it light.

8	large portobello mushrooms, stems removed, cleaned with a soft brush (do not wash); substitute other mushrooms, if necessary
16	chanterelle mushrooms, cleaned with a soft brush (do not wash); substitute other mushrooms, if necessary
2	tablespoons pure olive oil
2	tablespoons minced garlic
	Salt and pepper
4	cups mizuna greens, rinsed well and dried (substitute any peppery greens, like arugula or watercress)
	White Truffle Vinaigrette (page 208)
¼	cup sage leaves, cut into chiffonade

Preheat the oven to 350° F.

In a large mixing bowl, gently toss the mushrooms with the olive oil and garlic and season to taste with salt and pepper. Place in a single layer in an ovenproof baking dish and bake until tender, about 10 minutes.

In a large bowl, toss the mizuna with 4 tablespoons of the white truffle vinaigrette. Season to taste with salt and pepper.

Mound the greens in the middle of a large serving platter. Slice the portobello mushrooms thickly on the bias and arrange them around the greens; top with the chanterelles. Sprinkle with the sage leaves and drizzle with the remaining vinaigrette.

Saffron Rice Salad with Sweet and Fiery Dressing

Make this colorful vegetable salad on a base of saffron-perfumed rice. I like to add asparagus and roasted peppers, but you can put in your favorite vegetables or whatever looks best at the market. Serve at room temperature (see color pages).

FOR THE SAFFRON RICE

2 tablespoons (¼ stick) butter
½ onion, diced
2 tablespoons minced garlic
2 cups converted white rice
1 tablespoon saffron threads
4 cups water
1 tablespoon salt

Melt the butter in a medium saucepan over medium heat and sweat the onion and garlic about 4 minutes. Add the rice and stir to combine.

Add the saffron, water, and salt, raise the heat to high, and bring to a boil. Reduce the heat, cover, and simmer 20 minutes. Remove from the heat and allow to cool to room temperature.

FOR THE SALAD

Saffron Rice
20 asparagus spears, blanched and cut into 2-inch pieces (page 44)
3 yellow bell peppers, roasted, peeled, seeded, and diced (page 44)
3 red bell peppers, roasted, peeled, seeded, and diced (page 44)
1½ cups Sweet and Fiery Dressing (page 198)

In a large serving bowl, combine the rice with the asparagus and peppers. Pour the dressing over and mix.

Tarragon Cracked Wheat Salad

This citrusy salad of cracked wheat (bulgur), fresh bell peppers, tarragon, and honey goes well with grilled meats. Since it's served at room temperature, you can prepare it ahead of time and let it sit while you do the grilling.

1 **pound cracked wheat (bulgur)**
2 **red bell peppers, stemmed, seeded, and diced**
2 **yellow bell peppers, stemmed, seeded, and diced**
½ **cup coarsely chopped fresh tarragon**
1 **cup fresh lemon juice**
2 **tablespoons honey**
Salt and pepper

Cover the wheat with boiling water and let stand 15 minutes. Drain.

In a large bowl, combine the wheat, peppers, tarragon, lemon juice, and honey. Season to taste with salt and pepper.

Cabbage and Green Bean Salad

MAKES 8 SERVINGS

Here is the perfect accompaniment to crispy softshell crabs (see color pages).

- 1 **medium head of red cabbage, finely shredded**
- ½ **pound haricots verts**
- 1 **medium head of napa cabbage, finely shredded**
- 1 **jalapeño pepper, minced**
- 1 **cup rice wine vinegar**
- 3 **tablespoons pure olive oil**
- 1 **tablespoon honey**
  - **Salt and pepper**
- ¼ **cup Citrus Vinaigrette (page 203)**

Preheat the oven to 450° F.

In a large pot of boiling, salted water over high heat, blanch the red cabbage until wilted, about 1 minute. Shock in a bowl of ice water and squeeze dry. In a second pot of boiling, salted water over high heat, blanch the haricots verts until softened, about 1 minute. Shock in a bowl of ice water and drain. (Do not blanch the napa cabbage.)

In a large mixing bowl, combine the blanched and raw cabbage, jalapeño pepper, vinegar, oil, and honey; season to taste with salt and pepper. Transfer to a baking dish, cover with foil, and bake until cooked through, about 10 minutes.

Place in a serving bowl, toss with the citrus vinaigrette, and fold in the haricots verts. Serve at room temperature.

Spanish Potato Salad

Saffron, tomato, and thyme give a Latin flavor to this time-honored salad.

24 new potatoes, about 3 pounds
1 cup Saffron Mayonnaise (page 218)
1 medium tomato, coarsely chopped
1 tablespoon minced garlic
½ medium Spanish onion, diced
2 tablespoons fresh thyme leaves
¼ cup coarsely chopped flat-leaf parsley
Salt and pepper

Cook the potatoes in a large pot of boiling, salted water until tender, about 20 minutes. Drain and slice ½ inch thick. Place in a large serving bowl and keep warm.

In a mixing bowl, using a spatula, combine the mayonnaise with the tomato, garlic, onion, thyme, and parsley. Season to taste with salt and pepper. Pour the mixture over the warm potatoes and fold gently to combine.

Oven-Baked Eggplant and Manchego Cheese Salad with Fresh Oregano and Balsamic Glaze

MAKES 8 SERVINGS

Eggplant and melted cheese, layered into sandwiches, provide a delicious surprise in this salad. Manchego, made from sheep's milk, is one of the best-known Spanish cheeses, with great melting quality and just enough sharpness to contrast with the mild eggplant.

6 medium baby Italian eggplants, about 4 ounces each, sliced ⅛ inch thick

¼ cup pure olive oil
Salt and pepper

½ pound manchego cheese, sliced paper thin (if necessary, substitute another mild sheep's milk cheese, like provolone)
About ⅓ cup fresh oregano leaves, plus extra for garnish

1 teaspoon ancho chile powder (available at Hispanic or specialty markets)

2 cups balsamic vinegar

Preheat the oven to 425° F. Arrange the eggplant slices on a baking sheet, brush lightly with oil, and season to taste with salt and pepper. Bake until cooked through, about 8 minutes, without turning. Let cool at room temperature.

Arrange 8 eggplant slices on the baking sheet. Top each with a slice of cheese, sprinkle with oregano, and season to taste with salt and pepper. Top with another eggplant slice and sprinkle with ancho chile powder. Repeat with the remaining eggplant slices. The stacks can be refrigerated up to 1 day. Before serving, bake the eggplant in a 400° F. oven until heated through, about 10 minutes.

Bring the balsamic vinegar to a boil in a medium saucepan over medium-high heat. Reduce it by about four-fifths, until syrupy. Reserve at room temperature in a squeeze bottle or small bowl.

To serve, cut the eggplant stacks in half diagonally and arrange on a serving platter. Drizzle with the balsamic vinegar and garnish with oregano leaves.

Spicy Jumbo Lump Crabmeat and Black Bean Salad with Roasted Red Pepper Sauce and Cilantro Oil

MAKES 8 SERVINGS

More Cuban than Spanish, this salad of black beans and jumbo lump crabmeat is flavored with spicy peppers. It makes a spectacular presentation layered in an immense bowl and surrounded with bright green Cilantro Oil.

FOR THE BLACK BEANS	**1** pound dried black beans, picked over (or substitute 5 to 6 cups canned black beans)
	2 medium red onions, minced
	1 jalapeño pepper, minced
	6 tablespoons Citrus Vinaigrette (page 203)
	2 tablespoons pure olive oil
	1 teaspoon ancho chile powder (available at Hispanic or specialty markets)
	Salt and pepper

Place the beans in a large pot with cold water to cover and let stand overnight or for 8 hours. Drain the beans and again add cold water to cover. Bring to a boil over high heat, then reduce the heat to medium and simmer until tender, about 1 hour. Drain and reserve.

In a mixing bowl, combine the beans, onions, jalapeño pepper, vinaigrette, oil, and ancho chile powder. Season to taste with salt and pepper. May be refrigerated, covered, up to 1 day; bring to room temperature before serving.

FOR THE ROASTED RED PEPPER SAUCE	**4 red bell peppers, roasted, peeled, and seeded (page 44)** **½ medium red onion, coarsely chopped** **1 canned chipotle pepper** **6 tablespoons fresh lime juice** **1½ cups pure olive oil** **Salt and pepper**

In a blender, combine the bell peppers, onion, chipotle, and lime juice and blend until smooth. With the motor running, add the olive oil in a thin stream until emulsified. Season to taste with salt and pepper. Makes about 2 cups. May be refrigerated up to 2 days. Bring to room temperature before serving.

FOR THE CRAB	**2 pounds jumbo lump crabmeat, picked over** **4 tablespoons Roasted Red Pepper Sauce** **1 tablespoon fresh lime juice** **2 teaspoons honey** **1 tablespoon pureed canned chipotle pepper** **½ cup coarsely chopped cilantro** **Salt and pepper**

In a mixing bowl, combine the crab, red pepper sauce, lime juice, honey, chipotle puree, and cilantro. Season to taste with salt and pepper. May be refrigerated up to 1 day.

TO SERVE	**Roasted Red Pepper Sauce** **Cilantro Oil (page 210)**

Make a layer of black beans in a large serving bowl and top with a layer of crabmeat. Dress with the roasted red pepper sauce and spoon or squirt cilantro oil around the salad.

Sea Scallop Ceviche with Grilled Red Onion and Mango–Tortilla Salad

Contrary to what many people think, ceviche does not mean raw seafood—citrus juices "cook" the sea scallops enzymatically. The sweet scallops, juicy mangoes, grilled onion rings, and crisp fried tortillas give this beautiful dish lots of color and texture.

Everything in this salad can be done ahead: grill the onions, fry the tortillas, dice the mangoes, and marinate the scallops up to 1 day before serving, and combine all the ingredients at the last minute (see color pages).

24	large sea scallops, about 1½ pounds, halved lengthwise
2	cups fresh orange juice
2	cups fresh lime juice
2	cups fresh lemon juice
2	medium red onions, peeled and cut into thick slices
2	cups peanut or canola oil
6	blue corn tortillas, cut into fine julienne
2	small mangoes, peeled and diced
4	tablespoons finely chopped chives
2	tablespoons honey
	Citrus Vinaigrette (page 203)
	Salt and pepper
2	medium limes, peeled and sectioned
2	medium oranges, peeled and sectioned

In a bowl, combine the scallops with the orange, lime, and lemon juices. Refrigerate, covered, for 2 hours or up to 1 day.

Prepare a grill or preheat the broiler. Grill or broil the onion slices until just marked, about 2 minutes for each side. Reserve at room temperature.

Heat the oil in a large sauté pan over medium-high heat until it begins to smoke and fry the tortilla strips until crisp, about 30 seconds. Drain on paper towels.

Just before serving the scallops, drain off as much citrus juice as possible and add the mangoes, chives, honey, citrus vinaigrette, and salt and pepper to taste. Gently mix in the lime and orange sections, being careful not to break them.

To serve, place the onion rings in the center of a large platter and, using them as support, stand the tortillas in the middle. Surround with the scallop and fruit mixture. Sprinkle with pepper and serve immediately.

Octopus and Chickpea Salad

MAKES 8 SERVINGS

Octopus is kind of an exotic food, so a lot of people haven't tried it and haven't a clue about the best way to cook it. It is denser and thicker than squid, and you can't just throw it on the grill quickly—it will come out tougher than rubber. You have to simmer it for 2 hours, then refrigerate it in an herbal, citrusy marinade for another 8 hours, and finally, grill it just before serving. Sure, it sounds like work, but the result is worth it.

FOR THE OCTOPUS	3 **quarts water**
	3 **octopus, about 4 pounds**
	2 **cups red wine**
	2 **celery stalks, roughly chopped**
	2 **carrots, roughly chopped**
	2 **onions, roughly chopped**
	8 **bay leaves**
	Salt and pepper
	Juice and rinds of 4 lemons
	2 **cups pure olive oil**
	2 **heads of garlic, peeled and crushed**
	4 **rosemary sprigs, roughly chopped**
	2 **bunches of parsley, roughly chopped**

One day before serving, bring the water to a boil in a large pot. Add the octopus, wine, celery, carrots, onions, bay leaves, and salt and pepper to taste and bring to a simmer over medium heat. Continue simmering, uncovered, until the octopus is very tender, about 2 hours.

Remove from the broth and cool at room temperature. When cool, remove and discard the head and the stringy skin from the tentacles and cut the meat into chunks.

Combine the lemon juice and rinds, olive oil, garlic, and herbs in a small bowl and mix well.

Pour the marinade over the cooked octopus in a large bowl and refrigerate overnight or for 8 hours.

TO SERVE	**6 cups drained canned chickpeas** **Lemon Vinaigrette (page 199)** **Octopus** **Salt and pepper** **16 cherry tomatoes** **1 cup parsley leaves**

Combine the chickpeas with 1 cup of the vinaigrette. Set aside.

Prepare a grill and preheat the oven to 500° F.

Season the octopus with salt and pepper to taste and grill until hot. Grill the cherry tomatoes until they begin to blister, 10 to 15 seconds.

Toss the chickpeas and tomatoes and place on a large serving platter. Arrange the grilled octopus on top and drizzle with the vinaigrette, reserving any remaining vinaigrette to serve on the side. Garnish with the parsley.

Squid, Fried Plantain, and Mango Salad with Fresh Mint

MAKES 8 SERVINGS

Fresh mint isn't used often in savory dishes, but you find it that way in Cuban food. Here, in the cooling vinaigrette, it ties together several different notes: soft and buttery squid, crisp fried plantains, and sweet mango. This is another great salad where you can do all the components ahead and throw everything into a bowl at the last minute. Be sure not to overcook the squid (see color pages).

2	cups peanut oil
2	green plantains, peeled and sliced very thin on a mandoline or by hand
12	whole squid, skinned and cleaned
	Pure olive oil
	Salt and pepper
2	ripe mangoes, peeled and diced
4	cups arugula leaves
	Fresh Mint and Smoked Chile Vinaigrette (page 201)
1	red bell pepper, seeded and diced
12	fresh mint leaves, cut into chiffonade

Prepare a grill.

Heat the peanut oil in a large skillet over high heat to 375° F., or until a bit of bread sizzles on contact, and fry the plantain slices in batches until crisp. Drain on paper towels and reserve.

Brush the squid with olive oil, season to taste with salt and pepper, and grill for 3 minutes on each side. Alternatively, heat 2 tablespoons olive oil in a large skillet over medium-high heat until smoking and sauté the squid until golden on all sides. Cut into halves or 2-inch pieces.

Toss the squid, mangoes, and arugula with the vinaigrette in a large bowl. Season to taste with salt and pepper. Heap the salad onto a large platter and garnish with the fried plantains, diced bell pepper, and mint leaves.

Grilled Squid and Vidalia Onion Salad with Roasted Tomatoes and Green Chile Vinaigrette

MAKES 8 SERVINGS

Versatile, delicious, inexpensive squid is appreciated by almost every culture. This dish is sort of Mexican, adding Vidalia onions for sweetness (instead of fruit, as you might find in a Cuban-inspired recipe), along with tomatoes, some green chiles for heat, and a cool garnish of fresh mint.

FOR THE ROASTED TOMATOES	1 tablespoon pure olive oil
	4 plum tomatoes, halved
	Salt and pepper

Preheat the oven to 350° F. and lightly oil a baking sheet. Rub the tomatoes with olive oil, sprinkle with salt and pepper, and place cut-side up on the baking sheet. Roast 20 to 30 minutes, or until soft. Seed and dice the tomatoes.

	16	whole squid, skinned and cleaned
		Salt and pepper
	4	medium Vidalia onions, sliced ¼ inch thick
		Pure olive oil, for brushing
FOR THE SALAD	1	pound arugula
	1	pound frisée, washed and dried well
		Green Chile Vinaigrette (page 206)
	4	plum tomatoes, roasted, seeded, and diced
	12	fresh mint leaves, cut into chiffonade

Prepare a grill. Season the squid with salt and pepper to taste. Brush the squid and onions with olive oil.

Grill the squid 3 minutes on each side. Cut into halves or 2-inch pieces. Grill the onions on both sides until tender.

Combine the squid, arugula, frisée, and onions in a large serving bowl. Toss with the vinaigrette and top with the tomatoes and mint.

Carpaccio of Beef with Oregano Vinaigrette, Arugula, and Manchego Cheese

MAKES 8 SERVINGS

For this carpaccio, you need a perfectly fresh piece of beef that doesn't have a lot of fat. Filet mignon is the easiest cut to use but it's also the most expensive, so try top round—it has more flavor and costs less. The paper-thin slices of meat, with arugula, Oregano Vinaigrette, and a little manchego cheese for a Latin touch, make a dish with lots of interesting flavors running through it (see color pages).

FOR THE BALSAMIC REDUCTION	2 cups balsamic vinegar

Bring the balsamic vinegar to a boil in a medium nonreactive saucepan over medium-high heat and reduce it to ½ cup. Place in a squeeze bottle or small bowl and reserve at room temperature or refrigerate up to 5 days.

FOR THE BEEF

Beef round or top round, 20- to 24-ounce piece, completely frozen
Pure olive oil, for brushing
1 pound arugula, cleaned
Oregano Vinaigrette (page 198)
Salt and pepper
8 ounces manchego cheese, sliced paper-thin (if necessary, substitute another mild sheep's milk cheese, like provolone)
Balsamic Reduction

Slice the beef as thin as possible, place between 2 pieces of wax paper or plastic wrap that you have brushed with oil, and pound paper-thin with a mallet.

In a small mixing bowl, toss the arugula with 6 tablespoons of the vinaigrette and season to taste with salt and pepper.

Place the arugula in the center of a serving platter. Arrange the beef and cheese around it and drizzle with the remaining vinaigrette and the balsamic reduction. Season to taste with salt and pepper and serve immediately.

Red and Yellow Gazpacho with Grilled Sea Scallops

MAKES 8 SERVINGS

This is a play on classic gazpacho using red and yellow tomatoes. The yellow are sweeter than the red, so there is a good balance in the tomato flavors. The scallops add their sweetness as well as a smoky taste from the grill, but you can substitute grilled shrimp, if you prefer, or just leave the soup ungarnished (see color pages).

FOR THE GAZPACHO	
2	large yellow tomatoes, peeled, seeded, and diced
2	large red tomatoes, peeled, seeded, and diced
1	medium red bell pepper, seeded and diced
1	medium yellow bell pepper, seeded and diced
1	medium red onion, diced
3	cucumbers, peeled, seeded, and diced
¼	cup lime juice
¼	cup red wine vinegar
2	cups tomato juice
3	garlic cloves
6	slices of good-quality white bread
	Salt and pepper
16	Grilled Sea Scallops

In a large bowl, combine the tomatoes, bell peppers, onion, half the cucumbers, the lime juice, vinegar, and tomato juice.

In a food processor, puree the remaining cucumbers with the garlic and bread. Add the puree to the tomato mixture and season to taste with salt and pepper.

Serve in a large bowl, garnished with the sea scallops. May be refrigerated up to 1 day without the garnish, but it is best served within 2 hours.

FOR THE GRILLED SEA SCALLOPS	**16 large sea scallops** **¼ cup pure olive oil** **Salt and pepper**

Prepare a grill or preheat the broiler.

Rub the scallops with the olive oil and season to taste with salt and pepper. Grill or broil 2½ minutes on each side. Arrange on top of the gazpacho and serve immediately.

Vinaig

Oils,

Sauces,

and

rettes,

I love bold dishes composed of lively ingredients that play off one another, at times contrasting and at times blending. To tie together all the elements—some hot, some cool, some wilder than others—I bring out colorful herbal and citrus oils and vinaigrettes. And I add fragrant sauces and crisp relishes to supply even more color, flavor, and texture.

Using one or more of these in or alongside a dish is a great way to reinforce its predominant flavors, as well as to introduce new ones. Herbal, garlicky roasted chicken becomes even better when it is served with roasted garlic sauce, and sensational when it is drizzled with a little white truffle oil. Crushed Blackberry–Ancho Sauce provides the perfect contrasting finish for juicy pan-roasted rabbit (page 108), and Mango–Green Onion Salsa does the same for Potato and Cascabel–Crusted Halibut (page 112). All the oils, vinaigrettes, and sauces in this chapter can be drizzled over dishes, as well as served in small bowls alongside them. Each is a lot more than a garnish; it is an essential part of the whole.

Relishes

Flavored oils are an easy way to infuse notes of garlic, herbs, or chile into many dishes, and aromatic Garlic Oil comes with a bonus of crisp Toasted Garlic Chips. Store your oils in squeeze bottles so they will be easy to add to salads and to drizzle over and around roasted vegetables or fish. Most can be refrigerated up to 3 days but run the risk of spoiling after that.

Vinaigrettes add several flavors at once to a dish—sweet, sour, herb, and olive, for starters—and besides, they can be mixed in a flash in your blender. When you make them, follow these few rules to ensure success:

■ The classic ratio for vinaigrettes is 3 parts oil to 1 part vinegar, but don't be afraid to rebel against it a little. Many of my vinaigrettes require just a bit more acidity.

■ Use a blender for mixing because it will whip in some air and provide the best consistency.

■ After blending the ingredients, pour the vinaigrette into a plastic squeeze bottle. This will give you control when you add it to a salad or drizzle it over grilled fish or roasted vegetables.

■ When you dress a salad, especially when the greens are delicate, squirt or spoon the dressing around the sides of the bowl and just push the greens up into it. That way they won't be overdressed and soggy.

■ You can refrigerate most vinaigrettes up to 2 days. After that, they start to break down.

I include vinaigrettes or sauces used as marinades, such as the Garlic and Hot Pepper Marinade (page 82) for grilled steak or the Red Chile Marinade (page 84) for grilled pork tenderloin, in the appropriate chapter. The ones that follow are served alongside or drizzled over a finished dish, or used in more than one dish.

Bowls of bright sauces and relishes highlight the flavors of many things you serve, so don't limit them. Set them strategically around your table for guests to match with any foods they choose. You may even want to prepare extra vinaigrettes, oils, or sauces that aren't called for in any of the recipes but will add just the right dash of flavor to many of them. Glistening in small bowls, they will be beautiful visual accents to your table as well.

Sweet and Fiery Dressing

MAKES $\frac{1}{2}$ TO $\frac{3}{4}$ CUP

Serve with Saffron Rice Salad (page 174) or any rice.

1 tablespoon red wine vinegar
Juice of 3 limes
½ cup extra-virgin olive oil
¼ cup cilantro leaves
3 tablespoons honey
1 tablespoon pureed canned chipotle pepper
Salt and pepper

Combine the vinegar, lime juice, oil, cilantro, honey, and chipotle puree in a blender and blend until well mixed. Season to taste with salt and pepper and pour into a squeeze bottle. May be refrigerated up to 2 days. Bring to room temperature before using.

Oregano Vinaigrette

MAKES ABOUT 1 CUP

Serve with Carpaccio of Beef (page 190) or any grilled fish or meat.

¾ cup pure olive oil
¼ cup sherry vinegar (I prefer aged Spanish)
2 tablespoons honey
1 shallot, coarsely chopped
¼ cup fresh oregano leaves
Salt and pepper

Combine the oil, vinegar, honey, shallot, and oregano in a blender, and blend until well mixed. Season to taste with salt and pepper and pour into a squeeze bottle. May be refrigerated up to 2 days. Bring to room temperature before using.

Lemon Vinaigrette

MAKES ABOUT 4 CUPS

Serve with Octopus and Chickpea Salad (page 184) or any shellfish.

1 cup fresh lemon juice
1 cup sherry vinegar
4 tablespoons minced shallots
4 tablespoons minced garlic
1 cup parsley leaves
2 tablespoons thyme leaves
2 cups extra-virgin olive oil
Salt and pepper

Put the lemon juice in a small nonreactive pan over medium-high heat.

Combine the lemon syrup, vinegar, shallots, garlic, parsley, thyme, and oil in a blender and blend until well mixed. Season with salt and pepper to taste and pour into a squeeze bottle. May be refrigerated up to 2 days. Bring to room temperature before using.

Black Olive Vinaigrette

MAKES 1 1/2 CUPS

Serve with Grilled Salmon (page 95), Sweet Potato and Pine Nut Risotto (page 161), roasted rabbit, or any fish or poultry dish.

> **1** **cup pure olive oil**
> **2** **tablespoons red wine vinegar**
> **1/2** **cup seeded niçoise olives**
> **1** **teaspoon chile de arbole powder (available at Hispanic or specialty markets)**
> **2** **teaspoons finely chopped garlic**
> **1** **teaspoon Dijon mustard**
> **Honey**
> **Salt and pepper**

Combine the oil, vinegar, olives, chile powder, garlic, and mustard in a blender and blend until well mixed. Season with honey, salt, and pepper to taste and pour into a squeeze bottle. May be refrigerated up to 2 days; if not using immediately, leave out the garlic and add just before using. Serve at room temperature.

Fresh Mint and Smoked Chile Vinaigrette

MAKES ABOUT 1 CUP

Serve with Squid, Fried Plantain, and Mango Salad with Fresh Mint (page 186) or any grilled lamb dish.

¼ cup rice wine vinegar
⅓ cup extra-virgin olive oil
1 teaspoon pureed canned chipotle pepper
1 tablespoon honey
¼ cup fresh mint leaves, cut into chiffonade
2 tablespoons chopped cilantro
Salt and pepper

Combine the vinegar, oil, chipotle puree, honey, mint, and cilantro in a blender and blend until well mixed. Season with salt and pepper to taste and pour into a squeeze bottle. May be refrigerated up to 2 days. Bring to room temperature before using.

Rioja Red Wine Vinaigrette

MAKES 1½ CUPS

To make this vinaigrette, first reduce the red wine down to a concentrated syrup. The resulting small amount of syrup will be as filled with intense flavor as the wine itself. Serve with Skewered Lamb (page 88).

1 bottle Rioja red wine
¼ cup red wine vinegar
2 tablespoons Dijon mustard
1 teaspoon honey
1 cup pure olive oil
  Salt and pepper

In a medium saucepan over high heat, reduce the wine to about ¼ cup. Place it in a blender with the vinegar, mustard, and honey. With the motor running, slowly add the oil until emulsified. Season with salt and pepper to taste and pour into a squeeze bottle. May be refrigerated up to 2 days. Bring to room temperature before using.

Citrus Vinaigrette

MAKES ABOUT 2³/₄ CUPS

Citrus Vinaigrette is an important addition to Lump Crabmeat and Black Bean Salad (page 180), Sea Scallop Ceviche (page 182), and Cabbage and Green Bean Salad (page 176). But splashed over any kind of grilled fish, it will bring out all the natural flavors.

¼ **cup fresh orange juice**
¼ **cup fresh lemon juice**
¼ **cup fresh lime juice**
2 **fresh basil leaves, cut into chiffonade**
1 **tablespoon finely chopped red onion**
2 **cups pure olive oil**
Salt and pepper

Combine the juices, basil, and onion in a blender and blend until smooth. With the motor running, slowly add the oil until emulsified. Season to taste with salt and pepper. May be refrigerated up to 1 day. Bring to room temperature before using.

Spicy Orange Vinaigrette

MAKES 1 1/2 CUPS

Orange juice reduced to a syrup gives this vinaigrette a highly concentrated citrus flavor, delicious with Grilled Pork Tenderloin (page 84) or Almond-Crusted Cod (page 116), or over any grilled fish.

- 2 cups fresh orange juice
- 1/4 cup sherry vinegar (I prefer aged Spanish)
- 2 teaspoons Dijon mustard
- 2 teaspoons ancho chile powder (available at Hispanic or specialty markets)
- 1 cup pure olive oil
  Salt and pepper

In a medium nonreactive saucepan over high heat, reduce the orange juice to about 1/4 cup. Let it cool slightly.

Combine the orange syrup, vinegar, mustard, and ancho chile powder in a blender and blend 30 seconds. With the motor running, slowly add the oil until the dressing emulsifies. Season to taste with salt and pepper and pour into a squeeze bottle. May be refrigerated up to 1 day. Bring to room temperature before using.

Anchovy Vinaigrette

MAKES ABOUT 3 CUPS

Serve with fried squid or any grilled or roasted fish.

- 1 heaping tablespoon prepared mayonnaise
- 3/4 cup sherry vinegar
- 1 3/4 cups pure olive oil
- 8 anchovy fillets
- 2 shallots, finely diced
  Salt and pepper

Combine the mayonnaise, vinegar, oil, anchovies, and shallots in a blender or food processor and blend until smooth. Season with salt and pepper to taste and pour into a squeeze bottle. May be refrigerated up to 2 days. Bring to room temperature before using.

Green Onion Vinaigrette

MAKES ABOUT 2 CUPS

Serve with Saffron Risotto with Grilled Shrimp (page 156) or any grilled or roasted fish or poultry.

> 8 **scallions**
> ½ **large white onion, cut into chunks**
> 3 **garlic cloves**
> ⅓ **cup rice wine vinegar**
> 1 **cup pure olive oil**
> 1½ **teaspoons honey**
> **Salt and pepper**

Blanch the scallions for 30 seconds in a large pot of boiling salted water over high heat. Drain and shock in cold water.

Combine the scallions, onion, garlic, and vinegar in a blender and process until pureed. With the motor running, slowly add the oil until emulsified. Add the honey, season to taste with salt and pepper, and pour into a squeeze bottle. May be refrigerated up to 2 days. Bring to room temperature before using.

Green Chile Vinaigrette

MAKES 1 1/2 CUPS

Serve with Grilled Squid and Vidalia Onion Salad (page 188) and any grilled or roasted poultry or vegetables.

- **1 poblano pepper, roasted, peeled, and seeded (page 44)**
- **4 roasted garlic cloves (page 44)**
- **6 tablespoons red wine vinegar**
- **¾ cup pure olive oil**
- **Honey**
- **Salt and pepper**

Puree the poblano pepper and garlic with the vinegar in a blender. With the motor running, slowly add the oil until emulsified. Add honey and salt and pepper to taste and pour into a squeeze bottle. May be refrigerated up to 2 days. Bring to room temperature before using.

Sherry Vinaigrette

Use aged Spanish sherry vinegar if you can find it; regular sherry vinegar makes an acceptable substitute if you can't.

Serve with Bolo Salad (page 170) or any salad of your choice.

1/4 cup sherry vinegar (I prefer aged Spanish)
1 tablespoon Dijon mustard
1 cup extra-virgin olive oil
1 teaspoon honey
Salt and pepper

Combine the vinegar and mustard in a blender and process until mixed. With the motor running, slowly add the oil until emulsified. Add the honey and salt and pepper to taste and pour into a squeeze bottle. May be refrigerated up to 2 days. Bring to room temperature before using.

White Truffle Vinaigrette

MAKES 1 CUP

I love the flavor and the perfume of truffles, but their texture doesn't do anything for me. To capture the truffle essence, I use a fragrant oil that has been made by infusing ends or pieces in fine olive oil. This truffle oil is expensive, but a little goes a long way. Use it to finish white truffle vinaigrette rather than as the primary oil.

Serve this vinaigrette with Wild Mushroom and Mizuna Salad (page 172), or try it with roasted mushrooms, any vegetable risotto, or any chicken dish.

> 2 **tablespoons chopped shallots**
> ¼ **cup balsamic vinegar**
> 1½ **teaspoons Dijon mustard**
> ¾ **cup extra-virgin olive oil**
> 2 **tablespoons white truffle oil (available at specialty food shops and some supermarkets)**
> **Salt and pepper**

Puree the shallots in a blender with the vinegar and mustard. With the motor running, slowly add the olive oil and process until emulsified. With the motor still running, add the white truffle oil. Season to taste with salt and pepper. May be refrigerated up to 2 days. Bring to room temperature before using.

Balsamic-Mustard Vinaigrette

MAKES ABOUT 1 1/2 CUPS

This is my most basic vinaigrette and it works beautifully with all sorts of greens. Use it for Sophie's Salad (page 171) or any salad.

6 tablespoons balsamic vinegar
2 teaspoons Dijon mustard
1 cup pure olive oil
Salt and pepper

Combine the vinegar and mustard in a blender. With the motor running, slowly add the oil until emulsified. Season to taste with salt and pepper. May be refrigerated up to 2 days. Bring to room temperature before using.

Chile Oil

Serve with Oven-Roasted Wild Mushrooms with Goat Cheese (page 74) or any roasted vegetables.

1 cup pure olive oil
2 dried New Mexico chile peppers (available at Hispanic or specialty markets), stemmed and seeded
½ teaspoon dried chile de arbole (available at Hispanic or specialty markets)
1 teaspoon ancho chile powder (available at Hispanic or specialty markets)

Place all the ingredients in a blender and puree. Strain through a fine strainer. May be refrigerated up to 3 days. Serve at room temperature.

Cilantro Oil

MAKES ABOUT 2 CUPS

Certain herbs, such as basil, have to be blanched before they can be turned into herbal oils, but cilantro doesn't require that extra step. Because cilantro oxidizes slowly, this oil will stay a beautiful bright green. This is wonderful with Spicy Jumbo Lump Crabmeat and Black Bean Salad (page 180) and over grilled or roasted fish.

2 cups pure olive oil
3 cups packed cilantro leaves
Salt and pepper

Combine the oil, cilantro, and salt and pepper to taste in a food processor and process until smooth. Strain through a fine strainer and keep in the refrigerator. May be refrigerated up to 2 days. Use at room temperature.

Garlic Oil and Toasted Garlic Chips

MAKES 1 CUP GARLIC OIL AND 1 CUP
GARLIC CHIPS

Two separate condiments come from this one preparation. Serve the aromatic Garlic Oil in a small bowl for guests to dip their bread into and sprinkle these crisp garlic chips on top of Oven-Roasted Shrimp (page 69).

The paper-thin garlic slices are cooked very slowly so that, little by little, they become brown and crisp. They poach, rather than fry, in medium-hot olive oil.

1 cup pure olive oil
8 garlic cloves, peeled and sliced paper-thin

In a medium skillet over medium heat, heat the oil until it begins to shimmer. Add the garlic and cook until the slices begin to brown and curl. Remove with a slotted spoon and drain on paper towels. The chips may be kept at room temperature up to 1 day. Strain the garlic oil through a fine strainer and store in a squeeze bottle. The oil may be refrigerated up to 2 days. Use at room temperature.

Oven-Dried Tomato Oil

MAKES ABOUT 4 CUPS

Serve with grilled tuna marinated in romesco flavors with Melted Leeks and Onions (page 98) and over roasted or grilled vegetables or fish. This oil makes a beautiful accent for rice dishes.

> 6 plum tomatoes, halved lengthwise
> 3 cups plus 1 tablespoon pure olive oil
>   Salt and pepper
> 1 tablespoon chopped fresh thyme leaves
> ½ cup roasted garlic (page 44)
> ½ cup ancho chile powder (available at Hispanic or specialty markets)
> 2 tablespoons honey

Preheat the oven to 200° F.

Place the tomatoes cut-side up on a baking sheet. Brush with 1 tablespoon olive oil, season to taste with salt and pepper, and sprinkle with thyme. Roast overnight or for 8 hours.

Place the tomatoes in a saucepan over high heat with the remaining olive oil and bring to a boil. Pour the mixture into a blender, add the garlic, ancho chile powder, and honey, and process until smooth. Season to taste with salt and pepper and pour into a squeeze bottle. May be refrigerated up to 2 days. Use at room temperature.

Pomegranate Sauce

MAKES 3 TO 4 CUPS

Try this intensely flavored pomegranate sauce with a Thanksgiving turkey (page 60) instead of the traditional gravy, or serve it with any poultry or lamb.

Pomegranate seeds are like little red jewels. Add them to the sauce at the very last minute so they stay beautiful.

¼ **cup (½ stick) butter**
1 **medium Spanish onion, diced fine**
3 **tablespoons minced garlic**
2 **tablespoons whole black peppercorns**
1 **cup port wine**
6 **cups Chicken Stock (page 46; do *not* use canned)**
2 **cups pomegranate juice (available at specialty food stores or supermarkets), or substitute cranberry juice**
3 **tablespoons pomegranate molasses (available at Indian markets), or substitute regular molasses or honey**
2 **tablespoons light brown sugar**
Salt and pepper
4 **tablespoons finely chopped chives**
½ **cup pomegranate seeds**

Melt the butter in a large saucepan over medium heat and sweat the onion and garlic until the onion is tender, about 3 minutes. Add the peppercorns and cook another 3 minutes.

Add the port and cook, stirring, until most of it has evaporated. Add the stock, pomegranate juice, molasses, and brown sugar, raise the heat to medium-high, and reduce slowly to a sauce consistency. As the sugars caramelize, the sauce will turn brownish red. Season to taste with salt and pepper.

Remove from the heat. May be refrigerated up to 3 days. Reheat over medium heat. Fold in the chives and pomegranate seeds just before serving.

Crushed Blackberry–Ancho Sauce

MAKES ABOUT 4 CUPS

Serve with Pan-Roasted Rabbit (page 108) and with loin of lamb or lamb chops.

**FOR THE
ANCHO PUREE**

3 ancho chiles
4 cups boiling water
1½ teaspoons minced garlic
1 tablespoon chopped fresh cilantro

Combine the anchos and water in a small bowl and let stand 30 minutes or up to 8 hours. Drain well, reserving the soaking liquid. Remove the seeds and stems and puree in a food processor with the garlic, cilantro, and about ½ cup of the liquid, or as needed. Makes 1 cup. May be refrigerated up to 2 days.

FOR THE SAUCE

4 tablespoons (½ stick) butter
2 celery stalks, diced fine
1 medium carrot, diced fine
2 small yellow onions, diced fine
2 tablespoons black peppercorns
1 cup port wine
1 cup red wine
1 cup cranberry juice concentrate
½ cup ancho chile puree
4 tablespoons dark brown sugar
4 cups Chicken Stock (page 46)
   Salt
1 cup fresh blackberries

Melt the butter in a medium or large nonreactive saucepan over medium heat. Sauté the celery, carrot, and onions until the celery and carrot are tender and the onions are translucent, about 7 minutes. Add the peppercorns and continue cooking 2 more minutes.

Add the port, red wine, cranberry juice concentrate, ancho puree, sugar, and stock, stirring constantly and making sure to scrape the bottom of the pan. Cook until the mixture is reduced by half, strain, and season to taste with salt.

May be refrigerated up to 2 days. Reheat over medium heat. When ready to serve, fold in the berries.

Red Chile–Mustard Sauce

MAKES ABOUT 1 1/2 CUPS

Serve with yellow corn–coated softshell crabs (page 118) or any grilled chicken. This is a make-and-serve sauce that you can't refrigerate.

- **1 tablespoon butter**
- **1 small Spanish onion, finely diced**
- **1 tablespoon minced garlic**
- **2 tablespoons pasilla chile powder (available at Hispanic or specialty markets)**
- **3 tablespoons ancho chile powder (available at Hispanic or specialty markets)**
- **1/4 cup white wine**
- **1 cup heavy cream**
- **1/4 cup whole grain mustard**
- **Salt and pepper**

In a medium saucepan over medium heat, melt the butter and sauté the onion and garlic with the chile powders until the onion is soft, about 7 minutes. Make sure to stir constantly so the chile powders don't burn.

Add the wine and cook an additional 3 minutes. Add the cream and bring to a boil. Reduce the heat, add the mustard, and simmer 15 minutes. Season to taste with salt and pepper and serve immediately.

Mesa Barbecue Sauce

MAKES 2 CUPS

The sweet flavors balance the bold in this smooth sauce that comes from Mesa Grill, my New York Southwestern restaurant. Serve with Barbecued Baby Chicken (page 89), or use it to give magnificent flavor to any tender piece of meat.

2	tablespoons (¼ stick) butter
½	medium red onion, finely diced
3	garlic cloves, minced
6	plum tomatoes, coarsely diced
¼	cup ketchup
3	tablespoons dark molasses
2	tablespoons Dijon mustard
2	tablespoons dark brown sugar
1	tablespoon honey
1	teaspoon cayenne
1	tablespoon ancho chile powder (available at Hispanic or specialty markets)
1	tablespoon pasilla chile powder (available at Hispanic or specialty markets)
1	tablespoon paprika
1	tablespoon Worcestershire sauce

In a large saucepan over medium heat, melt the butter and sweat the onion and garlic until translucent, about 3 minutes. Add the tomatoes and simmer 15 minutes. Add the remaining ingredients and simmer 20 minutes.

Puree the mixture in a food processor, pour into a bowl, and let cool at room temperature. May be refrigerated up to 1 week or frozen.

Salsa Verde

Serve with Roasted Monkfish (page 71). Triple the recipe to serve with the Lobster Pan Roast (page 120).

4	tablespoons pure olive oil
3	tomatillos, papery skins removed, roughly chopped
2½	tablespoons coarsely chopped parsley
2½	tablespoons coarsely chopped basil
2½	tablespoons coarsely chopped tarragon
2	tablespoons water
1	teaspoon minced garlic
½	cup white wine
4	cups clam juice
	Juice of 1 lemon
	Salt and pepper
1½	tablespoons butter

Heat 2 tablespoons of oil in a medium sauté pan over high heat until almost smoking and sauté the tomatillos 3 minutes.

Place the tomatillos in a food processor, add the parsley, basil, tarragon, and water, and puree.

Place the remaining 2 tablespoons of oil and the garlic in a medium sauté pan over low heat and cook the garlic until cooked through.

Raise the heat to medium, add the wine, and reduce the mixture to almost dry, 3 to 4 minutes. Add the clam juice and reduce by four-fifths, an additional 5 minutes.

Add the lemon juice and season to taste with salt and pepper. Add the butter and the tomatillo-herb puree, taste, and reseason if necessary. The salsa should be full flavored. May be refrigerated up to 2 days. Use at room temperature.

Mango–Green Onion Salsa

MAKES ABOUT 2 CUPS

*Serve with Potato and Cascabel–Crusted Halibut (page 112)
or any fish.*

> 2 cups coarsely chopped mango
> 6 tablespoons finely sliced green onion
> 2 teaspoons minced jalapeño pepper
> ¼ cup fresh lime juice
> ¼ cup chopped cilantro
> Salt and pepper

Combine all the ingredients in a bowl, seasoning to taste with
salt and pepper. May be refrigerated up to 1 day. Bring to room
temperature before using.

Saffron Mayonnaise

MAKES 1 ¼ CUPS

*Use Saffron Mayonnaise in Spanish Potato Salad (page 177), and serve
with Batter-Fried Potatoes (page 128), grilled fish, or fish in broth.*

> ¼ cup red wine vinegar
> 1 tablespoon honey
> 2 pinches saffron threads
> 1 cup good-quality mayonnaise
> 1 teaspoon minced garlic
> Salt and pepper

Combine the vinegar, honey, and saffron in a small pot. Bring to a boil over high heat; immediately remove from the heat and let sit until cooled to room temperature.

Combine the mayonnaise and garlic with the saffron mixture in a small mixing bowl and season to taste with salt and pepper. May be refrigerated up to 2 days.

Red Onion Marmalade

MAKES ABOUT 3 CUPS

Dark magenta in color, this marmalade has a little bit of sweetness that mellows its underlying tart flavor. It's just a beautiful thing to have on the table.

Serve with Spicy Maple-Glazed Pork Chops (page 66) or any pork, beef, or chicken dish.

> 3 tablespoons butter
> 5 medium red onions, sliced thin crosswise
> 1½ cups red wine vinegar
> ½ cup crème de cassis
> ½ cup grenadine
> ½ cup red wine
> ½ cup coarsely chopped cilantro
> Salt and white pepper

In a large saucepan over medium heat, melt the butter and sweat the onions for 3 minutes, until soft. Add the vinegar, cassis, grenadine, and wine and reduce until the liquid has almost entirely evaporated and the onions are glazed, about 30 minutes. Add the cilantro and season to taste with salt and pepper. May be refrigerated up to 5 days. Use at room temperature.

Black Olive Tapenade

MAKES 2 CUPS

Use for Oven-Roasted Pork Tenderloin (page 64) and Tapenade-Crusted Salmon (page 115). I like to make this relish with some fresh garlic to bounce off the sweetness of the pineapple and oranges.

> 3 tablespoons pine nuts
> 1½ cups pitted niçoise olives
> 4 garlic cloves, peeled
> 3 anchovy fillets
> ¼ cup pure olive oil
> Salt and pepper

Place the pine nuts, olives, garlic, anchovies, and oil in a food processor and blend until the mixture is thick but still has texture. Season to taste with salt and pepper. May be refrigerated up to 3 days. Use at room temperature.

Orange-Pineapple Relish

MAKES ABOUT 4 CUPS

Serve with Grouper Roasted in Banana Leaves (page 70) or any shellfish or roasted or grilled fish.

> 1 cup fresh pineapple, cut into small dice
> 2 cups fresh orange segments
> ½ cup chopped red onion
> 1 New Mexico red chile, toasted in a pan over high heat for 20 seconds and crushed
> 1 teaspoon minced garlic
> 1 teaspoon honey
> 4 fresh mint leaves, cut into chiffonade
> 2 tablespoons extra-virgin olive oil
> Juice of 2 limes
> Salt and pepper

Combine all the ingredients in a large bowl and season to taste with salt and pepper. Let sit at room temperature for 30 to 45 minutes before serving. May be refrigerated up to 1 day.

Grilled Pepper and Black Olive Relish

MAKES 3 CUPS

Lots of Spanish flavors are joined in this dish, starting with roasted red peppers in combination with black olives. Serve with Garlic and Oregano–Marinated Grilled Chicken (page 90) or any grilled chicken or fish.

- **2 grilled red bell peppers, peeled, seeded, and diced**
- **2 grilled yellow bell peppers, peeled, seeded, and diced**
- **1 cup pitted and coarsely chopped niçoise olives**
- **2 tablespoons minced garlic**
- **¼ cup fresh thyme leaves**
- **½ cup coarsely chopped parsley**
- **¼ cup sherry vinegar (I prefer Spanish)**
- **2 tablespoons honey**
- **Salt and pepper**

Combine the peppers, olives, garlic, thyme, parsley, vinegar, and honey in a mixing bowl. Season to taste with salt and pepper. May be refrigerated up to 1 day. Use at room temperature.

Spicy Tomato Relish

Serve with Lobster Pan Roast (page 120) and Grilled Salmon with Sherry Vinegar–Honey Glaze (page 94).

- **2 medium ripe tomatoes, coarsely chopped**
- **2 tablespoons finely diced Spanish onion (or substitute white onion)**
- **1 tablespoon coarsely chopped parsley**
- **1 tablespoon red pepper flakes**
- **¼ cup red wine vinegar**
- **¼ cup pure olive oil**
- **Salt and pepper**

Combine the tomatoes, onion, parsley, red pepper flakes, vinegar, and oil in a mixing bowl and season to taste with salt and pepper. May be refrigerated up to 1 day. Use at room temperature.

Yellow Pepper Relish

Smooth and crunchy, this relish combines the textures of both diced and pureed peppers.

- **4 yellow bell peppers, roasted, peeled, seeded, and diced (page 44)**
- **4 yellow bell peppers, roasted, peeled, seeded, and pureed in a food processor (page 44)**
- **½ cup sherry vinegar (I prefer Spanish)**
- **1 tablespoon coarsely ground black pepper**
- **1 tablespoon honey**
- **¾ cup coarsely chopped fresh chives**
- **Salt**

In a mixing bowl, combine the diced and pureed peppers, vinegar, black pepper, and honey. Fold in the chives and season to taste with salt. May be refrigerated up to 1 day. Serve at room temperature.

Roasted Pepper Relish

MAKES 3 CUPS

This is a sparkling combination of sweet and hot peppers. Roasting takes away their raw flavor and softens them, as well as making them easy to peel.

Serve with Potato-Horseradish–Crusted Red Snapper (page 114) or any poultry or fish.

> 2 red bell peppers, roasted, peeled, seeded, and diced (page 44)
> 2 yellow bell peppers, roasted, peeled, seeded, and diced (page 44)
> ½ cup chopped black olives
> 1 tablespoon crushed red pepper flakes
> 2 tablespoons minced garlic
> 2 tablespoons fresh thyme leaves
> ½ cup chopped parsley
> ¼ cup sherry vinegar
> 2 tablespoons honey
> 6 tablespoons pure olive oil
> Salt and pepper

In a mixing bowl, combine the bell peppers, olives, pepper flakes, garlic, thyme, parsley, vinegar, honey, and oil. Season to taste with salt and pepper. May be refrigerated up to 1 day. Serve at room temperature.

Wild Mushroom–Roasted Corn Relish

MAKES ABOUT 4 CUPS

Take advantage of corn in its highest season with this great late-summer relish. Morels are delicious—but you can use creminis, all shiitakes, or any other mushrooms that tempt you. Serve with Barbecued Baby Chicken (page 89) or any pork or poultry dish.

4 tablespoons pure olive oil
1 cup quartered morels
1 cup shiitake mushroom caps
2 cups roasted corn kernels, from about 4 ears of corn (page 44)
4 teaspoons finely chopped jalapeño pepper
4 tablespoons fresh lime juice
½ cup coarsely chopped cilantro
2 teaspoons honey
Salt and pepper

Heat the oil in a medium sauté pan over medium heat until almost smoking and sauté the mushrooms until tender, 3 to 5 minutes.

Combine the corn, mushrooms, jalapeño, lime juice, cilantro, and honey in a bowl and season to taste with salt and pepper. May be refrigerated up to 1 day. Serve at room temperature.

Desserts
and Drinks

Look at dessert as a whole other gig—that's how I do it. To me, desserts are almost like a separate meal. You eat your dinner, you relax a little, and then later on, you enjoy the cake, ice cream, fruit, or flan. If you eat a meal straight through with no down time, in twenty-five minutes you're done and you're uncomfortable besides. I think the ideal interval between dinner and dessert is an hour and in that time, you can finish your wine or whatever you're drinking, maybe clear the empty platters and dishes, and sit around the table talking.

I love eating desserts, but I don't especially like making them —I'm not a pastry chef. So although my desserts are delicious, they tend to be pretty simple. This means that on my table you will find fresh fruit ices, an intense coffee ice cream, richly flavored flans and puddings, a cake filled with juicy apples, and a tart bursting with sweet, caramelized figs. Compared to a lot of fussy desserts, these are actually fun to do.

I've gotten a few good tips in my restaurant kitchens that help in the process. For instance, when you melt sugar down with a little water to make caramel, as in the Caramelized Fig Tart, you're not supposed to stir it more than one time. (My pastry chef, Wayne Brachman, says things like this that don't seem to make any sense but always work.) And when you scald milk and cream for a custard or a flan, don't mix it with the beaten eggs all at once. Add a little of the milk and cream mixture to the eggs to warm them, then pour them back into the milk. That is called tempering, and if you remember it, you won't scramble the eggs. Invest in a heavy-bottomed saucepan, especially if you are using an electric stove, so you won't burn your custards and sauces. Finally, measure carefully; even simple desserts require some precision.

Cold, slightly sweet sangria is my beverage of choice with Latin dishes. With sangria, you're not drinking a really serious bottle of red wine, you're drinking inexpensive but good-tasting wine that has been mixed with ripe fruits and mellow brandy. A couple of pitchers of this refreshing, fruity drink on the table send out the message of informality and fun. I include a sangria based on pomegranates for fall and one made with white peaches for summer.

Fresh Pineapple Ices

Don't puree the pineapple completely when you prepare these refreshing ices. This way, they will have an interesting texture, more like eating frozen pineapple. Make sure the pineapple you choose is fresh and ripe—you should be able to smell its sweetness when you pick it up (see color pages).

2 large ripe pineapples
½ cup water
1½ cups sugar

Peel, quarter lengthwise, and core the pineapple. Cut the quarters in half lengthwise, then into ¼-inch pieces.

Combine the water, sugar, and pineapple in a large saucepan and bring to a boil over medium heat. Stir, remove from the heat, and let cool.

Process the pineapple mixture to a rough puree in a food processor. Transfer to a shallow 1½-quart freezerproof container and freeze until hard, about 8 hours.

Just before serving, chop the ice into fine chunks with a fork or multipronged ice pick. Or place in the bowl of a strong mixer, like KitchenAid, and beat with the flat beater. Cover the bowl with plastic to keep the chunks from flying out. Place scoops of the ices in a large serving bowl.

Pomegranate Granita

Pomegranates are deliciously sweet and tart at the same time. The unusual flavor of the fruit makes you yearn for more—even while you're eating the granita.

Pomegranates can be juiced in a citrus juicer, or buy the juice in a health food store. Handle with nonreactive tools only (see color pages).

¼ **cup plus 2 tablespoons water**
¾ **cup sugar**
4 **cups pomegranate juice (approximately 8 large pomegranates)**

Bring the water and sugar to a boil in a small nonreactive saucepan over medium heat. Stir, remove from the heat, and let cool at room temperature.

Combine the syrup and pomegranate juice and transfer to a shallow 2-quart freezerproof container. Freeze 8 hours, stirring with a fork every 30 to 45 minutes, until set but granular. Or let the mixture freeze into a solid block, without stirring.

If necessary, just before serving, chop into fine chunks with a fork. Or place in the bowl of a strong mixer, like KitchenAid, and beat with the flat beater. Cover the bowl with plastic to keep the chunks from flying out. Place scoops of the granita in a large serving bowl.

Coffee Ice Cream with Cinnamon Buñuelos and Very Rich Chocolate Sauce

MAKES 8 SERVINGS

This dessert provides a pleasing contrast in texture between the smooth, thick ice cream and the crisp buñuelos. The flavors of coffee and cinnamon have great affinity for each other, so don't serve one without the other. Put scoops of ice cream into a big bowl surrounded by the crunchy cookies with their baked-in cinnamon topping.

FOR THE COFFEE ICE CREAM

- 1 tablespoon hot water
- 3 tablespoons instant espresso powder
- 2 cups whole milk
- 2 cups heavy cream
- 1 cup sugar
- 12 large egg yolks

Combine the water and espresso powder.

Scald the milk, cream, and 1 tablespoon of the sugar in a medium, heavy-bottomed pot over medium heat. Whisk the remaining sugar with the yolks and the coffee mixture in a large bowl until just blended. While constantly but very gently whisking the egg mixture, drizzle in the scalded milk mixture so that the eggs warm up gradually, without scrambling.

Pour the mixture back into the pot and cook over medium-low heat, stirring with a wooden spoon and making sure that you are constantly scraping the spoon across the pot bottom. The custard is done when it has thickened slightly (it will coat the back of a spoon and a line drawn across it with your finger will hold for 2 seconds).

Strain the custard into a bowl and place it in a larger bowl of ice. Stir occasionally until it has chilled, then freeze in an ice cream maker according to the manufacturer's directions. Transfer to a storage container and freeze until firm. It may be kept in the freezer up to 2 weeks.

FOR THE CINNAMON BUÑUELOS	6 **flour tortillas** **Canola or corn oil, for frying** 1 **teaspoon cinnamon** 2 **tablespoons sugar**

About 2 hours ahead, unwrap the tortillas and spread them out so they can dry. (This will prevent them from splattering when they are fried.) Place a 6-inch plate on 1 tortilla and cut around it with a sharp knife to form a 6-inch circle. Repeat with the other tortillas.

In a large skillet over high heat or in an electric fryer, heat 1 inch of oil to 375° F. Drop a tortilla in the oil and hold it submerged (use a pair of tongs) for 20 seconds. Continue to fry it until it turns golden brown and floats to the top, surrounded by a thin ring of tiny bubbles. Flip the tortilla over and fry the other side until lightly browned, about 30 seconds. Drain on paper towels. Repeat with the other tortillas.

Set a rack in the middle of the oven and preheat the oven to 350° F.

Place the tortillas on an ungreased baking sheet. Combine the cinnamon and sugar and sprinkle it on top. Bake until the sugar just melts, about 4 minutes. With a heavy knife, split the tortillas in half.

TO SERVE	**Very Rich Chocolate Sauce (page 248)**

Place scoops of the ice cream in a large serving bowl and drizzle on the chocolate sauce. Surround with the buñuelos. Serve any extra sauce on the side.

Pistachio-Phyllo Ice Cream Sandwiches with Very Rich Chocolate Sauce

MAKES 8 SERVINGS

Smooth, rich ice cream contrasts with crisp pastry and crisp-chewy pistachios in these unusual sandwiches drizzled with ultrarich chocolate sauce (see color pages).

FOR THE PISTACHIO ICE CREAM

- 1½ cups whole milk
- 1½ cups heavy cream
- ¾ cup sugar
- 9 large egg yolks
- 1 teaspoon vanilla extract
- ½ teaspoon almond extract
- 1 teaspoon rose water
- ¾ cup coarsely chopped pistachios

Scald the milk, cream, and 1 tablespoon of the sugar over medium heat in a medium heavy-bottomed sauce pot.

Meanwhile, whisk the remaining sugar, the egg yolks, vanilla and almond extracts, and rose water in a large bowl just to blend. While constantly but very gently whisking the egg mixture, drizzle in the scalded milk mixture so that the eggs warm up gradually, without scrambling.

Pour the mixture back into the pot and cook over medium-low heat, stirring with a wooden spoon and making sure that you are constantly scraping the spoon across the pot bottom. The custard is done when it has thickened slightly (it will coat the back of a spoon and a line drawn across it with your finger will hold for 2 seconds).

Strain the custard into a bowl and place it in a larger bowl of ice. Stir occasionally until it has chilled, then freeze in an ice cream maker according to the manufacturer's directions. When frozen, fold in the pistachios. Transfer to a storage container and freeze until firm. It may be kept in the freezer up to 2 weeks.

FOR THE PHYLLO SANDWICHES

8 sheets of phyllo pastry, thawed if frozen
3 ounces (³⁄₄ stick) butter, melted
Approximately 2 tablespoons sugar
Approximately ¹⁄₄ cup finely chopped pistachios
Very Rich Chocolate Sauce (page 248)

Set a rack in the middle of the oven and preheat the oven to 350°F.

Brush a sheet of phyllo with a thin coating of melted butter and sprinkle with approximately ³⁄₄ teaspoon of sugar and 2 teaspoons pistachios. Lay another sheet on top, brushing and sprinkling the same way. Repeat with a third sheet. Top with a fourth sheet and just brush with butter. Cut into 8 equal squares and transfer to a parchment-lined or nonstick baking sheet. Repeat the entire process with another set of 4 phyllo sheets.

Cover with a flat wire rack (this keeps the top of the pastry from floating off) and bake until lightly golden and crunchy, about 10 minutes. Cool at room temperature.

To serve, place a scoop of ice cream between 2 pieces of phyllo pastry and arrange the sandwiches on a large platter. Drizzle with the sauce.

Catalan Custard with Dried Fruits

This rich sherry- and vanilla-flavored dessert has a crisp topping of melted sugar, like a crème brûlée. Raisins and dried figs mixed into the custard and toasted almonds sprinkled over the top add a Spanish touch.

Bake the custard in an attractive ovenproof dish and bring it directly to the table. The custard can be made ahead of time and refrigerated, but caramelize the sugar topping at the last minute.

¼ **cup plus 2 tablespoons cream sherry**
¼ **cup plus 2 tablespoons water**
½ **cup raisins**
½ **cup coarsely chopped dried figs**
3 **cups heavy cream**
¾ **cup sugar, plus about ¼ cup for caramelizing**
1 **teaspoon vanilla extract**
8 **large egg yolks**
½ **cup lightly toasted sliced almonds (page 45)**

Set a rack in the middle of the oven and preheat the oven to 300° F.

Combine ¼ cup sherry, the water, raisins, and figs in a small saucepan over high heat and bring to a boil. Reduce the heat to medium and simmer 5 minutes. Let rest for at least 20 minutes.

Scald the cream and 1 tablespoon of the sugar in a medium, heavy-bottomed saucepan over medium-high heat.

Whisk together the remaining ½ cup plus 3 tablespoons sugar, 2 tablespoons sherry, the vanilla, and egg yolks in a large bowl until just blended. Whisking constantly but very gently, drizzle in the scalded cream. The egg mixture should warm gradually, without scrambling. Strain the custard into a pitcher.

Drain off any liquid that remains in the dried fruit and spread on the bottom of an 8-cup baking dish. Pour the custard over the fruit.

Place the baking dish in a roasting pan and fill the pan with hot water to come halfway up its sides. Tightly cover the pan with foil and bake until the custard jiggles slightly but its surface is smooth and set, 1 to $1\frac{1}{4}$ hours. Let cool to room temperature in the water, then remove from the roasting pan and refrigerate 4 hours or up to 2 days.

Before serving, preheat the broiler. Sprinkle a light layer of sugar on top of the custard and broil directly under the heat, watching very carefully, just until the sugar caramelizes. While the caramel is hot and sticky, sprinkle with the almonds. Wait a minute or two until the surface hardens and then serve.

Toasted Almond Flan

Toasted almonds add extra flavor and texture to a classic Spanish flan. Toasting the almonds brings out their natural flavors and oils, but be careful not to overcook them (see color pages).

FOR THE CARAMEL	¼ cup water 1 cup sugar

Cook the water and sugar in a small, heavy-bottomed saucepan over high heat stirring once, until syrupy and a light amber color. Immediately pour into a completely dry, shallow 6-cup baking dish. Taking care not to touch the hot syrup and stirring only once, swirl it to coat the inside of the baking dish halfway up.

FOR THE CUSTARD	1½ cups whole milk 1½ cups heavy cream ¾ cup sugar 3 tablespoons amaretto liqueur 4 large eggs 6 large egg yolks ½ cup (1¼ ounces) lightly toasted almonds (page 45)

Set a rack in the middle of the oven and preheat the oven to 300° F.

Scald the milk, cream, and 1 tablespoon of the sugar in a medium, heavy-bottomed saucepan over medium-high heat. Whisk the remaining sugar with the amaretto, eggs, and yolks in a large bowl just until blended. While constantly but very gently whisking the egg mixture, drizzle in the scalded milk mixture so that the eggs warm up gradually, without scrambling.

Strain the custard into a pitcher. Pour it into the baking dish and skim off any bubbles that have formed on the surface.

Put the baking dish into a roasting pan and fill with enough hot water to come halfway up the sides. Tightly cover the pan with foil and bake until the custard jiggles slightly but its surface is smooth and set, 1 to $1\frac{1}{4}$ hours.

To unmold, run a small, thin knife between the custard and the inside of the dish. Place a plate or platter upside down over the custard and flip both over sharply. If the custard doesn't come right out, shake it a few more times. Sprinkle with the toasted almonds. May be refrigerated up to 3 days.

Pumpkin Flan

MAKES 8 SERVINGS

Here is a perfect Thanksgiving dessert, with the fragrance and flavor of pumpkin and spice. True, it is rich, but on Thanksgiving that's allowed—you're expected to fall asleep forty-five minutes after you've finished eating. Because unmolding can be messy, with caramel spilling everywhere, serve the flan right from the baking dish.

Pumpkin is one of the few foods I will use out of a can. If you want to impress your friends, go ahead and buy a pumpkin and roast and puree it. But I find the canned vegetable to be consistently good—which is not true of the fresh. Unadorned, pumpkin doesn't have much flavor, so it needs to be spiced up with cinnamon, nutmeg, and a little clove or mace. (I always thought that pumpkin naturally tasted like this spice mixture until I tasted some that hadn't been seasoned. It was a little like zucchini.)

FOR THE CARAMEL

¼ cup water
1 cup sugar

Cook the water and sugar in a small, heavy-bottomed saucepan over high heat, stirring once, until the syrup turns a light amber color. Immediately pour the caramel syrup into a completely dry 8-cup baking dish. Taking care not to touch the hot caramel, swirl it to coat the inside of the baking dish halfway up.

FOR THE CUSTARD

1½ cups whole milk
1½ cups heavy cream
¾ cup sugar
1 teaspoon cinnamon
½ teaspoon ground cloves
1 cup pumpkin puree
¼ teaspoon freshly grated nutmeg
4 large eggs
6 large egg yolks

Set a rack in the middle of the oven and preheat the oven to 300° F.

Combine the milk, cream, and 1 tablespoon of the sugar in a small, heavy-bottomed saucepan over medium-high heat and bring just to a scald (listen for a hissing sound, like a cappuccino machine steaming milk).

Meanwhile, in a large bowl, combine the remaining $\frac{1}{2}$ cup plus 3 tablespoons of the sugar, the cinnamon, cloves, pumpkin, nutmeg, eggs, and yolks and whisk just to blend.

While gently whisking the egg mixture, drizzle the hot cream mixture into it so that it is gradually warmed. Strain the custard into a pitcher, then pour it into the prepared baking dish. Skim off any bubbles that have formed on the surface.

Put the dish in a roasting pan, add enough hot water to come halfway up the sides, and bake 1 to $1\frac{1}{4}$ hours. The custard is done when its surface is smooth and set but it jiggles slightly when gently shaken. Or stick a very small knife into the custard and pull it out slowly. If done, it will come out clean. If there is custard on it, continue cooking. If the custard is overcooked, you will see bubbles around the side. Let cool to room temperature in the water bath, then remove and refrigerate at least 8 hours or overnight. Serve in the baking dish.

Chocolate-Coconut Bread Pudding

MAKES 8 SERVINGS

Chocolate and coconut are a great combination that is Cuban in origin. These flavors make the pudding very sweet but not cloying. Grated coconut adds just a touch of texture.

¾	pound stale challah, brioche, or French bread, cut into ¾-inch cubes
6	ounces semisweet chocolate
1½	14-ounce cans coconut milk
1½	cups heavy cream
¾	cup sugar
9	large egg yolks
1½	cups shredded coconut

Set a rack in the middle of the oven and preheat the oven to 300° F. Place the bread cubes in a 2½-quart baking dish.

Melt the chocolate over barely simmering water in the top of a double boiler or in a small bowl fitted tightly into a saucepan.

Scald the coconut milk, cream, and 1 tablespoon of the sugar in a medium, heavy-bottomed saucepan over medium-high heat. Combine the remaining sugar with the egg yolks in a large bowl and whisk just until blended. Whisking constantly but very gently, drizzle in the scalded cream. The egg mixture should warm gradually, without scrambling. Whisk in the warm chocolate, then strain the mixture over the bread cubes. Stir gently until all the bread is soaked with custard.

Place the baking dish in a roasting pan and fill the pan with hot water to come halfway up its sides. Tightly cover the roasting pan with foil and bake until the pudding is barely set, 35 minutes. Remove the foil and sprinkle with the coconut. Bake just until the coconut is lightly browned and the custard is completely set, 8 to 10 minutes. It may be refrigerated up to 3 days; reheat at 300° F. before serving.

Caramelized Fig Tart

MAKES ONE 10-INCH TART SERVING 8 TO 10

In this variation of a traditional apple tart, ripe, fresh figs provide the luscious layer of caramelized fruit that is set on top of a crisp crust. This tart is best eaten the same day it is baked (see color pages).

FOR THE TART DOUGH

1 **cup all-purpose flour**
1 **tablespoon granulated sugar**
6 **tablespoons (¾ stick) cold butter cut into pea-sized bits**
1 **egg**
1 **cup ice water**

In a large bowl, whisk together the flour and sugar. Using either a pastry blender or your fingers, work in the butter until the mixture resembles coarse meal.

In a small bowl or measuring cup, combine the egg and ice water. Sprinkle 2 to 3 tablespoons of the egg mixture onto the flour mixture and mix it in with your fingers just until the dough masses together in a ball. Discard the leftover egg mixture.

On a lightly floured work surface, tear off egg-size pieces of dough and smear them away from you with the palm of your hand into 6-inch lengths. Scrape up the dough, pile the lengths on top of one another, and form into a disk. Wrap in plastic and refrigerate 2 hours or up to 8 hours.

On a lightly floured work surface, roll the dough into a 10-inch circle about ⅛ inch thick. Using a 10-inch plate as a pattern, trim the edges with a sharp knife. Transfer to a parchment-lined or nonstick baking sheet and refrigerate 1 hour.

2 pints fresh figs
½ cup confectioners' sugar
¼ cup granulated sugar
1 teaspoon ground cinnamon
6 tablespoons (¾ stick) butter, melted

Slice the figs ¼ inch thick. Mix the sugars and cinnamon together in a small bowl.

Set a rack in the middle of the oven and preheat the oven to 400° F.

Using the largest fig slices, form a ring ¼ inch from the inner edge of the pastry. Form another ring of slices inside the first. Using the smallest slices, make a final ring in the center of the tart. If there is space in the center, fill it with fig scraps.

Using a pastry brush, paint the figs with a thin coating of melted butter. Evenly sprinkle ¼ cup of the sugar mixture onto the tart or, for best results, tap the mixture through a small strainer.

Bake 10 minutes. Remove from the oven and sprinkle with another ½ cup of the sugar mixture. Paint again with the melted butter and bake for another 10 minutes, or until the bottom is lightly browned. Don't overbake, or the fig topping will run.

Bolo Roasted Apple Cake with Sherry Custard Sauce

MAKES 8 SERVINGS

The slight tartness of Granny Smith apples is mellowed by a touch of sherry, a flavor repeated in the rich custard sauce you spoon over slices of this cake. Roasting the apples ahead releases their delicious juices (see color pages).

FOR THE ROASTED APPLES

2 tablespoons cornstarch
¾ cup dark brown sugar
1 cup sherry (sweet, if possible)
1 teaspoon vanilla extract
6 large Granny Smith apples, peeled, cored, and cut into 8 wedges
Butter, for greasing the baking dish

Preheat the oven to 400° F.

Whisk together the cornstarch, brown sugar, sherry, and vanilla in a mixing bowl. Mix in the apples and pour into a 2-quart baking dish that has been greased with butter. Cover and bake 15 minutes, lifting the cover to baste a few times. When the liquid starts to jell, remove the cover and bake until slightly softened, 5 additional minutes.

FOR THE CAKE	1½ cups cake flour
	¼ teaspoon baking soda
	1 teaspoon baking powder
	¼ teaspoon salt
	½ cup (1 stick) butter, at room temperature
	1 cup granulated sugar
	2 eggs, at room temperature
	2 teaspoons vanilla extract
	2 tablespoons sherry
	¾ cup buttermilk, at room temperature
	Sherry Custard Sauce (page 249)

While the apples are baking, sift together the flour, baking soda, baking powder, and salt onto a sheet of wax paper. Sift 2 more times to mix and aerate.

Beat the butter and sugar at high speed with an electric mixer until well combined and smooth, about 2 minutes. Add the eggs and beat until light and fluffy, about 5 more minutes, scraping down the sides of the bowl as necessary. With the mixer on its lowest setting or by hand with a rubber spatula, fold in a third of the flour mixture. Fold in the vanilla, sherry, and half the buttermilk, then another third of the flour, then the remaining buttermilk. Finally, fold in the remaining flour mixture.

Cover the apples with the batter and bake until the cake is golden and the center springs back when lightly pressed, 30 to 35 minutes. Serve the sherry custard sauce alongside.

Very Rich Chocolate Sauce

Serve over coffee ice cream with Cinnamon Buñuelos (page 232) and with Pistachio-Phyllo Ice Cream Sandwiches (page 234).

1   cup heavy cream
4   ounces bittersweet chocolate, chopped into small
    chunks
½   cup Kahlúa (you may substitute framboise,
    amaretto, or Grand Marnier, or add another
    ½ cup heavy cream)

Scald the cream in a small saucepan over medium heat. Put the chocolate into a small bowl, pour half the hot cream over it, and gently stir to melt and blend. Add the remaining cream and the liqueur and stir until smooth. May be refrigerated up to 2 weeks.

Sherry Custard Sauce

MAKES 1³/₄ CUPS

Serve alongside Bolo Roasted Apple Cake (page 246).

½ cup whole milk
½ cup heavy cream
¼ cup sugar
3 egg yolks
¼ cup cream sherry, such as Harvey's Bristol
    Cream or Dry Sack
1 teaspoon vanilla extract

Scald the milk, cream, and 1 tablespoon of the sugar in a medium, heavy-bottomed pot over medium-high heat.

Whisk the remaining sugar, the yolks, and sherry in a small bowl just to blend. Whisking constantly but not vigorously, gradually drizzle in the scalded milk mixture so that the yolks warm without scrambling.

Return the mixture to the pot over medium to low heat and stir with a wooden spoon, making sure that you scrape the spoon across the pot bottom. The sauce will be ready when it has thickened slightly. (It will coat the back of the spoon. Draw a line through it with your finger. If the line holds for 2 seconds, the sauce is done.) Remove from the heat and add the vanilla. Cool at room temperature, then strain and refrigerate up to 3 days.

Bolo's Pomegranate Sangria

Pomegranate juice has a tart fall flavor that works beautifully in a traditional Spanish sangria, the refreshing combination of wine and ripe fruit. This drink goes with anything—have a pitcher of it on the table at all times.

- 2 **bottles dry white wine**
- ¾ **cup brandy**
- ½ **cup triple sec**
- ¾ **cup simple syrup (page 43)**
- ¾ **cup pomegranate juice (available at specialty markets)**
- 2 **oranges, sliced into thin rounds**
- 2 **green apples, cored and sliced thin**
- 2 **lemons, sliced into thin rounds**

Combine all the ingredients in a large pitcher and refrigerate, covered, 2 hours or up to 2 days. Serve over ice.

Bolo's White Peach Sangria

Summer brings white peaches, which complement white wine. Any time of year, peach nectar is a convenient substitute for the fresh fruit (see color pages).

- **2 bottles dry white wine**
- **¾ cup brandy**
- **½ cup triple sec**
- **¾ cup simple syrup, or more if needed (page 43)**
- **3 or 4 white peaches, skinned and pureed (¾ cup puree), or ¾ cup peach nectar (available at supermarkets)**
- **3 oranges, sliced into thin rounds**
- **3 green apples, cored and sliced thin**
- **2 lemons, sliced into thin rounds**
- **4 peaches, pitted and sliced thin**

Combine all the ingredients in a large pitcher. If using fresh peaches, taste for sweetness and add more syrup, if needed. Refrigerate, covered, 2 hours or up to 2 days. Serve over ice.

Index

RESOURCES

Tableware seen in the color photographs is available from the following:

HOLLOWBROOK POTTERY
26 Anton Place
Lake Peekskill, NY 10537
(914) 328-2434
*Honey-Rum Baked Black Beans
Lemon-Thyme Rice*

SIMON PEARCE
120 Wooster Street
New York, NY 10012
(212) 334-2393
Saffron Rice Salad with Sweet and Fiery Dressing; Carpaccio of Beef with Oregano Vinaigrette, Arugula, and Manchego Cheese; Red and Yellow Gazpacho with Grilled Sea Scallops

WOLFMAN GOLD & GOOD COMPANY
117 Mercer Street
New York, NY 10012
(212) 431-1888
All other tableware